WEATHER AND WARFARE

John Tyrrell lectures in the Geography Department
at University College Cork, is a Fellow of
the Royal Meteorological Society and member of
the Irish Meteorological Society. A contributor to
several books and journals on climatology,
he is the Irish co-ordinator of the European-wide Tornado
and Storm Research Organisation (TORRO).

Weather and Warfare

A Climatic History of the 1798 Rebellion

John Tyrrell

The Collins Press

PUBLISHED BY
The Collins Press, West Link Park, Doughcloyne, Wilton, Cork, 2001

British Library Cataloguing in Publication data.

ISBN: 1-898256-04-7

Printed in Ireland by Woodprintcraft Group

Jacket design by Artmark

CONTENTS

To Cesca
Jeremy and Amanda, Zoe and Martyn

FOREWORD

The bicentennial commemorations of the 1798 rebellion in Ireland gave a special opportunity for intense historical analysis of events that still reverberate in Ireland today. Our historians rose to this challenge and produced many new studies of the personalities, historical movements and the events of that time. As well as significant works of scholarship there were a considerable number of local studies that were the product of detailed research in particular historical landscapes by local historians and interest groups. These have rescued from obscurity an important local heritage that has now been made available to the wider community. It is my hope that such local studies will find an additional insight into their stories from the pages of this book.

This publication is not another history. Instead, it attempts to build on the foundation provided by the historians. Without their painstaking reconstruction of events and the analysis of the forces that lay behind them this present work would not have been possible. I have taken the results of their work and viewed them from quite a different perspective. As a climatologist I am convinced that the weather permeates the whole of life and as I have read various histories of late eighteenth-century Ireland and the political upheavals that occurred, I have seen suggestions here and there of the weather imposing itself at critical moments. Eventually I became so intrigued by these fragments that it became a compelling task to put together a fuller picture of the meteorological realities of that period and how they may have shaped some of the most important events.

However, this is not a new climatic determinism. It is an attempt towards a clear recognition that weather and climate play a complex, and sometimes direct, role in the lives of people, communities and even nations. More often than not it is an indirect role that is difficult to define, but that does not invalidate an attempt to identify it and make it explicit. The narrative method adopted in this account should help to achieve this. The heart of the book lies in the daily synoptic maps that are laid side-by-side with the narrative. Synoptic maps in the simplified form in which they are presented are an ideal tool with which to draw the historical and meteorological narratives together.

One of the most important reasons for studying the past is to gain insights into the present. This has become an important objective in studies of historical climates. As we transform our atmosphere by polluting it at an unprecedented rate, there is an increasing interest in considering what our weather and climate was in the recent past. This book had its origin in a wider search for historical sources of climatic data. It was hoped that these would contribute to extending the knowledge of our Irish climate backwards in time in a way that would permit comparisons with the present. The advent of the age of meteorological instruments in Ireland coincided historically with the turmoil of other revolutions that produced large amounts of contemporary documentation. Had it been a quiet period politically, no doubt this documentation would have been very slight. Instead, this revolutionary period has a richness and variety of source material that has made this study possible. I am sure there is much similar data waiting to be discovered, both for this period as well as earlier periods of the eighteenth century. Despite its variety, all of the material has a place in establishing the day-to-day synoptic weather conditions. It is these that ultimately must be at the heart of long-term climatic change studies, because people, plants, animals and whole environments respond to what they actually experience and encounter day-by-day rather than some abstract seasonal or annual mean.

My continuing work in this area owes a debt of gratitude to a bunch of Irish historians who gathered for a week in Bantry during the summer of 1997 to study the French expedition to Bantry in 1796. It was an inspirational week led by Professor John A. Murphy. Subsequently there was a lot of encouragement to engage with historical themes by Kevin Whelan, David Drew and Tom Dunne, who stimulated my ideas in many ways. Others have also played a significant role in bringing this to completion. The maps are at the heart of the publication, so it with deep gratitude that I acknowledge the hours (often very unsociable ones) of dedicated work by Mike Murphy to produce them. The co-operation and personal kindness of the present Lord Kilmaine in allowing access to his family papers are deeply appreciated. In addition, the ready assistance of John Butler at Armagh Observatory, the helpful staff of the Public Record Office at Kew, the Leicestershire County Library, the Linen Hall Library, the Royal Irish Academy and the Boole Library at UCC all made the necessary trawl through their archives a most pleasant experience. But the project was made much easier because of the wider assistance of friends and family as I travelled to archives and walked the landscapes of the rebellion in corners of Ireland that I would not otherwise have visited, in pursuit of information. To all of you, my deepest gratitude. Finally, the generous financial support of the Faculty of Arts Research and Publication Funds is gratefully acknowledged.

JOHN TYRRELL
CORK, 2001

1

HINDCASTING THE WEATHER OF 1798

Everyone is familiar with the weather forecast. Each day thousands of people across Ireland want to know what weather is likely to occur over the next few hours or days. This is a clear indication of how much the weather permeates our lives today. Our modern forecast is based on the careful analysis of observations gathered over a wide area. We can also look back in time and 'hindcast' the weather. A hindcast is really a work of detection, because it identifies weather conditions that have already occurred and are embedded in a vast array of information left from an earlier time. By combining these historical observations on a map the synoptic situation as it is likely to have been can be reconstructed. The further back in time we go to do this, the more diverse the information that must be used. For 1798 there is a richness of source material that makes this task possible.

MEMORY AND TRADITION: The Irish folk memory has left us echoes of the weather of 1798. It is not a strong memory but it is there. The legacy of folklore, poetry and song has ensured that graphic weather images of that rising have been ingrained indelibly into the history of 1798, weaving the details of the stage on which the events took place into the events themselves. The results are striking. Oral and other tradition records that:

'... '98 was a very dry year. I often heard that there never fell a shower of rain in this part from March to November', and, '... it was upon the whole one of the finest summers I have known, a great deal of calm, sunny, and fine weather, and moderately hot', and, 'the summer being remarkably fine and dry'.[1] So, it appears the high aspirations and memorable actions were carried out under idyllic conditions. This is almost fairy tale land, or the stuff of heroic epics.

Historians who have revisited and analysed the events have distilled these images into the record. They have concluded that, 'The weather throughout the rebellion was remarkably fine and warm'[2], 'it was the summer of the century'[3], 'the spring and summer had been very fine, with no rain falling for several weeks'[4] and have referred to 'that golden summer..'[5], 'an exceptionally long spell of dry weather'[6], 'the unusually dry weather'[7] and 'the exceptionally hot weather'.[8] All these quotations point to the variety of weather conditions that deserved special mention in the record. The dryness and heat receive most comment whilst the relative calmness of the wind also gets a mention. It is recognised that historians have shown some of their political biases in their analyses of 1798, yet bias is much less of a problem with regard to their weather references. Weather is normally mentioned in passing and is incidental to the main historical narrative. Therefore, the probability of weather descriptions being massaged for political ends is low. The greater difficulty is likely to arise from another source, namely the generalisations often made for the sake of simplicity.

Many of these weather images are now enshrined in poetry and song, written long afterwards. They have become our own mental pictures, having been handed down to us over the years. Memorable actions and weather are combined in the memory of Father John Murphy lighting the flame of rebellion at Boolavogue, County Wexford, as recorded in a song of the same name by P.J. McCall that opens with the words:[9]

> *At Boolavogue as the sun was setting o'er the bright May meadows of Shelmalier.*

A similar backcloth is recorded for some of the major actions. In the poem 'Mary Doyle, the Heroine of Ross', the scene before the action at New Ross is described by William Rooney:[10]

> *Through the misty morning by the hedgerows bright we sped,*
> *While the lark with joyous music filled the spreading dome o'erhead,*
> *And the sun rode up the circle, and the earth began to smile,*
> *But our hearts knew naught of pleasure, they were cold as ice the while.*

And later, the fighting continued:

> *Till the misty summer morning wore into the dusty day.*

The weather theme is the same in another poem by William Rooney that recorded the victory at Ballyellis in County Wicklow,[11]

We marked them on the plain that June day warm and still,
And lined the blossomed ditches twain on Ballyellis Hill.

In *Shemus O'Brien*, by Sheridan Le Fanu,[12]

The mornin' was bright, an' the mists rose on high,
An' the lark whistled merrily in the clear sky –

The short-lived northern rebellion began over two weeks later than the rising in Wexford, but its folk history also contains a memory of sunny days in Eithne Carberry's song called *Roddy McCorley*,[13]

The grey coat and its sash of green were brave and stainless then;
A banner flashed beneath the sun o'er the marching men –

A traditional air recalls the death of the northern leader, General Munro, who led the United forces at the decisive battle of Ballynahinch,[14]

'Twas early one morning when the sun was still low –
that they murdered our hero, brave General Munro;

The long-awaited and ultimately untimely invasion by the French came in late August. But the weather theme in song is virtually the same. In the song, *The Men of the West*, again by William Rooney, the scene is set,[15]

The hilltops with glory were glowing, 'twas the eve of a bright harvest
*   day,*
When the ships we'd been eagerly waiting, sailed into Killala's broad
*   bay;*

And in the following verse,

Killala was ours ere the midnight, and high over Ballina town,
Our banners in triumph were waving before the next sun had gone
*   down.*

Thus, in the events of the early summer and again at its end, the emphasis is on the good weather, and in particular the sun. This record has no claim to accuracy. However, it has struck a chord that resonates through the folk memory of 1798 that has helped to give us an impression of a summer with outstanding weather.

But there are other records of that summer that speak more clearly and more objectively about the weather. A number of weather registers that recorded daily observations were kept during 1798 and have survived to the present. In addition to these sources there are the records made on board the ships of contending navies along the sealanes of western Europe. Individually each of these records would be valuable in characterising the weather of 1798. But when put together, for locations extending from the Bay of Biscay to the North Sea and to the eastern Atlantic, as well as across the land surface of Ireland, it is possible to reconstruct entire weather patterns day by day. This provides an opportunity to examine both the accuracy of the folk memory and to explore the contribution the weather made to the significant events of the rebellion. The detailed nature of this study observes an important principle for examining the relationship between weather and its impact. That principle is that the time-scale of the weather information must relate to the time-scale of the events themselves. Thus, the weather's influence on the outcome of a battle or day-to-day strategy requires daily weather information.

LOGBOOKS: The most important source of information for this reconstruction was the logbooks maintained on board the ships of the British navy. Their importance lies both in the discipline of regular observational and recording requirements set by the Navy Board as well as the geographical distribution of the ships themselves. The officer responsible for making the logbook entry was the master of the ship who, under the captain, was responsible for its navigation. To do this he had to provide his own instruments, including a quadrant or sextant, as well as maps and books on navigation. His duties required him to gather hydrographic information for correcting coastal maps and noting offshore hazards, so he needed considerable observational skill and an attention to detail far above the average sailor.[16] The observations were made on a slate and kept up to date by the master's mate of the watch. The mate marked the slate which was then certified by the officer of the watch, if not the master. While under sail this was done every hour, although in port this was reduced to three times a day. The frequency of these observations make it possible to trace the passage of entire weather systems and to capture many details that would otherwise be lost. At noon the observation was done normally by the master himself when he would take a sighting of the sun (weather permitting), record the ship's position and note significant details of the weather. He would then enter the information into the logbook together with what was already on the slate.

This included information on wind direction and its strength, precipitation, visibility and cloudiness. As a warrant officer, the master stayed with his ship, even if it was laid up, and promotion was not common. Consequently, he knew intimately the behaviour of his ship and its response to different conditions, and logbook entries are normally reliable and consistent.

A second logbook was kept by the ship's captain. But, unlike the master, he was a commissioned officer, with a commission to serve on a ship for a specific period, after which he actually became unemployed (until he received a commission to another ship). He was required to keep a record that included the same observations as the master. But this record is intrinsically less useful as far as the weather is concerned. It was very common for the captain to copy the master's log. It is also probable that some masters made up both logbooks, as clearly indicated by the identical handwriting in both logbooks of the frigate *Magnanime*. As a result, the two logbooks do not always provide a separate accuracy check. Nevertheless, keen observation was at the heart of the routine and activities on board a frigate or ship of the line. This was no more evident than at the beginning of each day. In times of war, as in the 1790s, dawn would break with every navy vessel at sea at battle quarters in case the light revealed an enemy ship. They went to quarters fifteen minutes before dawn and two lookouts were sent aloft. Lookouts were posted at the masthead throughout the day, while during the night they were replaced by six lookouts on deck each watching a separate arc of the horizon. While the importance of wind direction and speed to the sailing of the ship was reason enough to ensure that it was noted with some care, a number of other routines on board were closely related to the weather in such a way as to give confidence in using the information. Rainfall, for example, was frequently recorded in the log. Besides its intrinsic importance as an element of the weather it affected the daily routine of the ship. Normally the upper deck would be scrubbed every morning and the lower decks once a week (normally Wednesdays), provided the weather was good enough to let the decks dry out quickly. Dampness was regarded as bad for health and for stores and provisions.

The frequent lack of independence between the master's and captain's logbooks calls for another method by which their information can be verified. This is readily to hand. Few ships travelled alone. Most were either in a squadron patrolling a section of the sea or providing protection for a convoy of merchant ships with one, but usually more, other navy vessels. As a result logbooks of accompanying ships can be checked against each other. Normally this results in data of the highest quality as well as an outstanding amount of detailed information.

In Ireland, the main harbour for the British navy was Cork. From 1794 vice-Admiral Kingsmill, an Irishman from County Donegal, had been in command there. His duties were to organise convoys, protect shipping off the Irish coast from pirate adventurers and watch out for the French.

Kingsmill's priorities appeared to be in that order, as he demonstrated in December 1796 when he largely discounted reports of a French invasion fleet being nearby.[17] His flagship, the 64-gun *Polyphemus*, spent most of its time in Cork harbour, particularly during the summer of 1798, so the logbook weather information compiled by its master William Langton can be mapped easily.[18] A number of other ships also had permanent or semi-permanent locations during the summer of 1798. In the same way their positions can be readily fixed for plotting their weather data. The logbook of the ship *Princess* is particularly important because the ship had been moored in Waterford harbour since the end of 1797 and was there throughout most of the Wexford rising.[19] It left for Cork on 14 June with numerous prisoners on board. In addition, a daily meteorological record for Dublin is provided by the navy's yacht *Dorset*, which was there for use by the Irish government.[20] It occasionally conveyed important messages or personnel to England, docking in the river Dee for rapid communication with London. At the other extremity of Ireland the frigate *Cerberus* was stationed in Lough Swilly until the end of July, and thereafter patrolled the western coast.[21] But most of the vessels whose logbooks were used for hindcasting purposes were at sea for the majority of the time. In all, the daily logbook records for the period between May and the end of October were extracted from the logbooks of 46 ships.[22] On any one day there were always at least fourteen (but often many more) that were suitably positioned to be used for constructing the day's synoptic chart. The positions of the ships varied, but they followed well-used routes, taking their bearings from adjacent coasts with familiar landmarks. Further out to sea they normally traced their course by dead reckoning, but their daily positions can still be established with confidence because they sailed in convoy or in squadrons and their records can be matched against one another (Fig 1.1).

There is one important area of the map where there is a gaping hole with no data. This is the open Atlantic to the west of Ireland. It is important because many of the weather systems approach Ireland

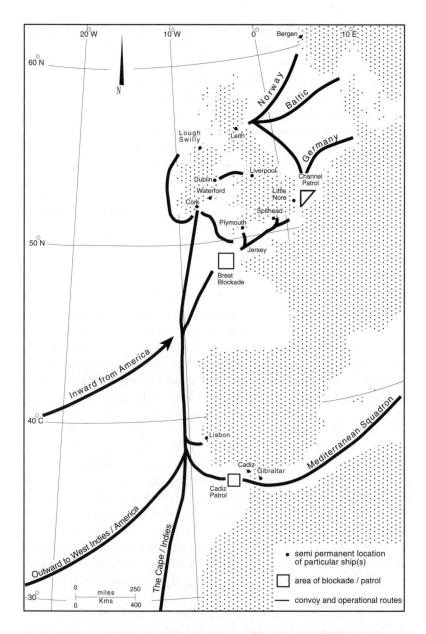

Fig 1.1. The principal ports and sea routes used by the ships of the British navy whose logbooks were used to construct weather hindcasts, May-October 1798.

from that direction. It would be wrong to assume that convoys heading to the colonies in North America took the most direct route and thereby provide weather data for the Atlantic approaches in their log-books. This would have been too risky. The ships would easily have got lost. Navigation depended on being able to view the skies, particularly when travelling in an east-west direction when an accurate determination of the ship's longitude was necessary.[23] Convoys would, therefore, gather in Cork, or at other harbours on the south coast, and then sail southwards, measuring their progress by observing their latitude. Having reached more southerly latitudes they then had the benefit of the clearer skies and calmer weather of the Azores and a following current and wind to cross the Atlantic. Their return route frequently followed a more northerly route, using the southern edge of the westerly winds to advantage, but it still resulted in an approach to Ireland or Britain more from the south than from the west. Thus, approaching depressions are not picked up in the maps of 1798 weather. Only their arrival is recorded.

INSTRUMENTAL OBSERVATIONS: The eighteenth century was a time of radical change. Not only was this change expressed in terms of the political and historical events that profoundly influenced the nature of Europe, but also in the science that was beginning to transform how the world was understood. Observation and measurement of the atmosphere was in its infancy. As it pushed beyond the folk understanding encapsulated in the weather lore of the day, across Europe individuals and groups were beginning to make regular observations. New instruments had been devised to measure pressure, temperature, humidity and other weather elements. These slowly spread where there were individuals with the curiosity, resources and opportunity to use them. In Ireland the age of meteorological instruments and scientific measurement was also dawning. This dawn was proving to be a long one. But eighteenth-century Ireland did see a few individuals beginning to use barometers and thermometers as they also observed the wind and weather. The result was a growing number of daily registers of weather, some of which are available for the study of 1798. Three particularly important Irish meteorological records stand out:

Armagh: One of the most significant sources of meteorological data for the historical study of weather in Ireland is the observatory in Armagh. It is the only site where meteorological observations were being made in the late eighteenth century that is still operational today. Because its 200-year record is unique in Ireland it is an important benchmark against which other shorter records are frequently matched. What made this different from other observatories that had an early birth was that its establishment by an Act of Parliament in 1790 gave it a permanent status rather than it being dependent upon an enthusiastic individual whose interest in recording the weather was not shared by successive generations.[24] In 1791, Rev Dr James Archibald Hamilton was the first to take up the position of Director and Astronomer at Armagh. He was uncle to the much more famous physicist and mathematician, William Rowan Hamilton of Dublin, and he was to have a profound effect upon young William's early education. It was under him that the first regular, systematic meteorological observations were made at Armagh, in 1795. Before his appointment there he had established an observatory at Cookstown and from his communications to the Royal Irish Academy in Dublin it is clear that as early as 1783 he was regularly using a barometer, thermometer and rain gauge as part of his meteorological observations.[25] He was also interested in extending the use of the principal meteorological instrument of the time, the barometer, by proposing modifications to make it much more portable.[26]

When he moved to Armagh it is, therefore, no surprise that he added meteorological equipment to the observatory and organised a detailed daily record of the weather. However, a rain gauge was not included. But precipitation was one of several meteorological conditions noted alongside the instrumental observations of atmospheric pressure and temperature. In using these data today, difficulties arise because of uncertainties with regard to the instrument design and exposure. These can be overcome by using the data as a measure of day-to-day changes in weather rather than trying to derive any absolute values of temperature and pressure based on various corrections. From that year temperature and pressure readings were recorded three times each day, at 8am, noon and 8pm.[27]

Belfast: Not too far away another weather register was being maintained, in Belfast.[28] To have a second set of daily observations relatively close to Armagh that can provide a check is a remarkably fortunate circumstance. For this record we must be grateful to successive librarians of the Linen Hall Library. Today the Linen Hall Library stands opposite the City Hall in the centre of Belfast. But in 1798, when it was known as 'The Belfast Library and Society for Promoting Knowledge', it was located where the City Hall now stands. As well as being a library for Belfast's citizens, it became noted for recording atmospheric phenomena and keeping a register of the weather. This was made possible by the early acquisition of two thermometers, two barometers, a rain gauge, hygrometer and an endiometer.[29] The library buildings formed a large open quadrangle and it was in the centre of this that the instruments were exposed. The one exception was the barometer, which was kept indoors.

The responsibility for the meteorological recordings fell to the librarians. The library regulations included '1. The Librarian shall ... keep a register of the weather'.[30] Each day meticulous care was required to make an accurate record in the weather register. Here, there is an interesting connection with the 1798 rising, as the librarian who was appointed in 1794, Thomas Russell, was an intimate friend of Wolfe Tone. Russell was politically very active and was a founder member of the United Irishmen. His journals reveal a wide interest in the environment, including geology and natural history, but he also expressed his political views by writing for the newspaper associated with liberal opinion in the north, the *Northern Star*. This was closed and its proprietors arrested in 1796. Russell was arrested at the same time, terminating his meteorological (and other) duties at the Library. He was immediately replaced by John McCoughtry, who remained as librarian until 1802. So it was McCoughtry who made the observations during the summer of 1798. Today, this meteorological record is intact with the exception of three days, from 11-13 June. These days were at the height of the rising in Ulster and a curfew was put in place throughout the city. As a result it was not possible to get to the Library and make the usual weather observations. However, it is fortunate that the Armagh record is intact for this period and the weather was fairly settled, so the gap is not critical. The main problem in using these data lies in the uncertainty over the timing of the observations. In 1802 it was at 2pm, and it is not certain whether the practice in earlier years was any different.

Kilmaine of Westmeath and Mayo: Meanwhile, on an estate in County Westmeath, another daily register of weather was being maintained by Lord Kilmaine. The existing record begins in 1794. But early in this record it is noted that a third new barometer was being used, so the use of such instruments to record the weather had been carried on for some time. John Kilmaine kept the record himself and it does, therefore, suffer from discontinuities caused by his journeys and travels. He partly overcame this by having instruments at both of his two main residences. One of these was at Neale in County Mayo and the other was at Gaulston in County Westmeath. However, when he travelled within Ireland, and particularly to Dublin, he was often unable to refer to his instruments at all, but he would carry his weather register with him and still manage to record a description of the weather each day. His practice was to divide the day into four periods (morning, noon, afternoon and evening) and describe the weather for each. His instruments consisted of a barometer and thermometer and he recorded their measurements, as well as wind information, just once during the day. All the evidence points to this being at midday. A particular exception to this practice was when he had to travel to England. One such period occurred in 1798. He set off for England on 8 February to attend to legal affairs in London and his daily record then has a gap until 1 July when he was back in Dublin. The date of his return to Ireland is uncertain because his journals for May and June are missing. As a result they provide no help in reconstructing the meteorological picture for the early period of the rebellion, and in particular the Wexford rising. But they do contribute a great deal of data from July onwards. Kilmaine spent most of August and September at his home in County Mayo, including the period of the French invasion, and then took up residence at Gaulston early in October. As well as taking a close interest in the weather his knowledge of plant and animal life on the one hand and astronomy on the other was extensive. His notes reflect a keen eye and a close attention to detail. Despite these genuine interests he appears to have had little connection with the fledgling Royal Irish Academy in Dublin, several of whose members were showing much interest in instrumental weather observations at this time. But they seem to have been unaware of Kilmaine's weather records.

The Royal Irish Academy. In Ireland there was a growing interest in meteorology during the late eighteenth century and, in particular, in making measurements with the new meteorological instruments that were becoming available from abroad. The Royal Irish Academy, founded in 1785, played a very important role in their dissemination. At its own expense it supplied numbers of these instruments to those it thought would use them. But few of the records that may have been made during the surge of enthusiasm for the new science appear to have survived to the present. The Academy had intended that the recipients of the instruments would communicate their observations. Only a few of them did so. For these the Academy provided a valuable focus and their observations were published in its proceedings in the form of monthly summaries. However, with regard to reconstructing the daily weather for 1798 this format limits their usefulness since day-to-day changes in the weather cannot be traced. Nevertheless, they do provide us with monthly trends that show how the summer weather progressed, as well as some of the contrasts that occurred across Ireland.

There were only three significant contributors of observations for 1798. Colonel William Paterson in Londonderry was a corresponding member of the Academy who not only kept a careful record of the weather but also of the instruments he used and their exposure.[31] He refers to his barometer as being 'that of the Academy', a clear indication that he had taken up its offer of equipment. His other instruments, a thermometer, hygrometer and rain gauge, may not necessarily have come from the same source. The second record comes from what must have been quite a remarkable young man. Henry Edgeworth of Edgeworthstown, County Longford, was a mere sixteen years old in 1798. This probably makes him the youngest Irish meteorological observer on record. Undoubtedly he benefited from the education provided by his older sister, Maria, who became a significant contributor to the development of educational ideas in Ireland. Their father, who was also an active member of the Academy, had given the responsibility for young Henry's education to Maria.[32] The record includes a description of the instruments used, although one suspects that this was a standard requirement of the Academy.[33] Finally, Richard Kirwan in Dublin was the main source of energy in this project. He became a significant figure in the development of Irish science.[34] But while he researched a variety of scientific questions, he also maintained his own set of meteorological instruments at his home in Cavendish Row (a barometer, thermometer and rain gauge). His observations were published from 1789, although it is very likely that he began at an earlier date.[35]

The hindcast: In Ireland, the value of mapping simultaneous observations of the weather and constructing a synoptic map for a large area was not realised in practice until 1851.[36] This can now be attempted for 1798 by combining the data recorded at sea with that on land, to produce a hindcast. This has been achieved through the construction of a synoptic map for each day of the period between mid-May and the end of October 1798.[37] The key to this task is the availability of wind and pressure observations. In studies of historical weather and climate it is sometimes overlooked that the wind pattern is a more fundamental feature of our atmosphere and its climate than the recorded temperature or the measured rainfall. These circulation patterns determine the nature of the air drawn across Ireland; whether, for example, it is arctic, polar or tropical air. In addition, the movement and interactions

of these different air types give rise to major rain-producing mechanisms, particularly frontal systems. The absence of measurable temperatures and quantities of rainfall does not prevent an accurate charac-
terisation of the weather that is directly comparable with modern
weather data.

To reconstruct each of the weather maps for 1798 the observations
made at noon were used. Once these data were checked against a
neighbouring ship (or site) the wind direction was plotted and the
pressure patterns for the area were determined, adding in the limited
barometric data where it was available. This pattern had to be consistent with the map for the preceding day so that day-to-day changes
were accurately portrayed. Other weather information derived from
the weather records was then incorporated (including temperature,
forms of precipitation, wind strength, clouds, visibility and sunshine).
Even twentieth-century weather maps were of some assistance.
Modern synoptic charts with a pressure pattern that closely resembled
the reconstructed 1798 map were consulted and comparisons made
with the weather information available for them. In this way a detailed
picture of the daily weather that probably occurred across Ireland on
particular dates was built up. The final maps that are depicted here
show a more limited area than the North Sea to North Africa area used
to construct the original maps. The smaller area makes Ireland sufficiently large to show the sites of the action in relation to the evolving
weather conditions.

2

MAY: THE BENEDICTION OF HEAVEN

The summer really began on 19 May with the arrival of an anticyclone from southern Europe. In Ireland, summer anticyclones are mostly associated with settled, dry, warm weather, and this was to prove no exception. Despite its persistence in the days ahead, small shifts in position produced changes of wind direction that were to play an important part in the unfolding conflict. The first wave of the rebellion broke out around Dublin, but the most important engagement during May was at Enniscorthy, in the centre of County Wexford. Its capture generated shock waves far afield. The evolving weather played a considerable part in the outcome of this battle, as well as in other events across the county.

Until 19 May the weather seemed unremarkable. Indeed, it had rained on many of the preceding ten days in most places as low pressure dominated the weather maps (Fig 2.1). But the rain was light and sufficient to encourage the growth of crops. Newspapers were already noting that the harvest prospects were good.[1] With rapidly rising pressure at Armagh the rain ended and the weather warmed.[2] By 25 May the midday temperatures were at 20^0C.[3] Increasingly after 22 May (on the south coast) and 24 May (in the north) the skies were clear and winds were light, making afternoon temperatures uncomfortably hot whenever there was little wind to relieve them.

By the end of May the weather was extremely pleasant. The positive outlook it encouraged among the insurgents was reinforced by prophecies that the good weather would remain until the rising was successful and that no rain would fall until they had finally conquered. This was a sign 'that the benediction of heaven rested on their cause' being 'sent by the Almighty to favour their cause'.[4] In the rebels' own words, 'God is on our side, the heretics have had dominion long enough, but our time is now come'.[5]

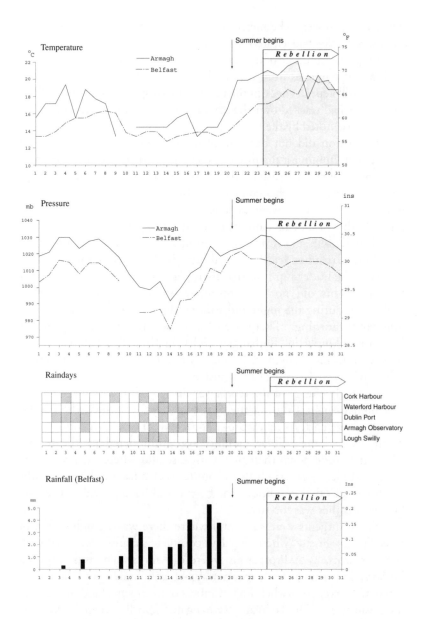

Fig 2.1. The beginning of the summer in terms of temperature, pressure, raindays and rainfall, May 1798.

MAY 23-24: THE REBELLION BEGINS IN LEINSTER

The day began well. The meteorological observer at Armagh noted that the overcast sky had cleared and that for once it was a bright, warm morning. The influence of the drifting anticyclone, then over Britain, was pushing light breezes from the south across Ireland (Fig. 2.2). But the heat was still kept in check in the east by clouds spreading inland. Where the breezes had tracked over the sea, as in the southeast, there was a fine weather haze noted by the master of the *Princess* in Waterford harbour.

The action did not begin until the evening when the daily mail coaches left Dublin for the provinces. It was planned that they would be seized and their non-arrival in towns along their routes was to be the signal for the rising. Coaches going to Belfast, Athlone, Limerick and Cork were seized, but others were not stopped.[6] The night's weather was ideal for ambush work, being cloudy and quite dark, yet dry and clear.

Near Dublin and in the counties of Kildare, Meath and Carlow, the United Irishmen had been well organised. But earlier pre-emptive arrests of the leadership thwarted their plans for Dublin and the wider province. This did not prevent many groups of United Irishmen mobilising during the night and striking during the early hours of the following morning. There were successes for the insurgents at Properous, Dunlavin, Rathangan and Old Killcullen (25 May), but reverses at Clane, Ballymore Eustace, Monasterevan, Naas and Carlow (25 May), as well as smaller skirmishes.

The early energy of the rebels was dissipated in a string of defeats and high casualties during the first two days, in which the cavalry played a large part. As rebels broke at the end of several encounters the cavalry were lethal. Their mobility was unhindered by the terrain where they rode down their prey with ease and where there were few places to hide. There was little to counter such a fast, mobile and ruthless force. In other conditions the bogs could have provided a refuge, but the weather was too dry.

The insurgents were successful where there was a combination of three factors. Firstly, where they had complete surprise combined with superior arms, as at Prosperous where captain Swayne was surprised indoors, killed and the garrison trapped and burnt out.[7] Secondly, where there were overwhelming numbers of insurgents (and no defending cavalry), as at Dunlavin and Rathangan.[8] Thirdly, where broken terrain and confined space cancelled out the cavalry, as at Old Killcullen.[9]

The dryness of the weather quickly became a factor, among others, in the conflict. From the beginning fire was used as a weapon and

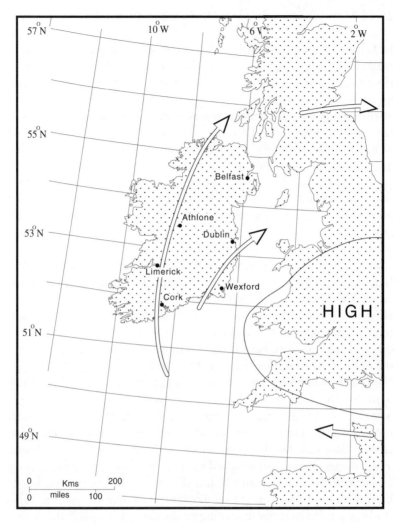

Fig 2.2. Synoptic weather map, 23 May.

the tinder-dry materials of buildings fuelled many an inferno. Numerous burnings were acts of retribution, carried out by both sides. But in pitched battles they were more often used to advantage by the insurgents, particularly where a garrison was under cover and the rebels could see no other means of overcoming it.

25-26 May: Under Open Skies in County Wexford

In County Wexford martial law had been declared on 27 April. This marked the beginning of a terrible time. The stories from other counties of arms searches and arrests accompanied by torture, murder and house burning were now experienced in the county and a sense of alarm verging on panic became widespread. A rumour that the yeomen (and in its wildest form, Protestants) were all Orangemen determined to massacre them was rife, and Cloney tells of whole villages emptying as people fled to the fields, woods and ditches to escape them.[10]

The centre of the anticyclone expanded on its western side while the winds remained very light and southerly (Fig. 2.3). This produced extremely pleasant weather during the day but it was also of considerable significance for the multitudes who had to spend these nights out of doors. There was sufficient moisture in the light southerly winds coming off the sea to produce thin cloud at night as the air cooled. Indeed, on 25 May, in Dublin, it was enough to produce some showers of rain during the day. But this appears to have been the exception. However, the overnight cloud retarded the usual night fall in temperature, so the nights were relatively mild. With little wind, weather conditions could not have been better for those driven to seeking refuge in the open air or who travelled at night to seek a safer refuge.[11]

Outdoor clothing was almost as important as the weather. A key item for the men was a long, loose, woollen coat known as the 'trusty'.[12] Although their size and weight made them cumbersome, unwieldy and an impediment to movement, it was worn over a waistcoat or close jacket with sleeves and short breeches open at the knees. Their owners became so attached to them that they could hardly ever be persuaded to take them off and dispense with them, even in the hottest summer. It was also a significant feature that the colour of this clothing tended to differ according to the district in which the wearer resided. In many of the sketches of events during the rebellion, the majority of insurgents are depicted wearing their 'trusty', for example, in the cartoons of George Cruikshank.[13]

The flight into the night and the fear of massacre reached a peak on Friday 25 May. The following day, possibly heartened by news of rebel successes in County Kildare, and further incensed by yeomanry outrages elsewhere, Fr John Murphy of Boulavogue led his local people to oppose a patrol of yeomanry cavalry in a skirmish during which two local yeomanry leaders were killed. The response was predictable. From Ferns and Enniscorthy new patrols fanned out in the evening

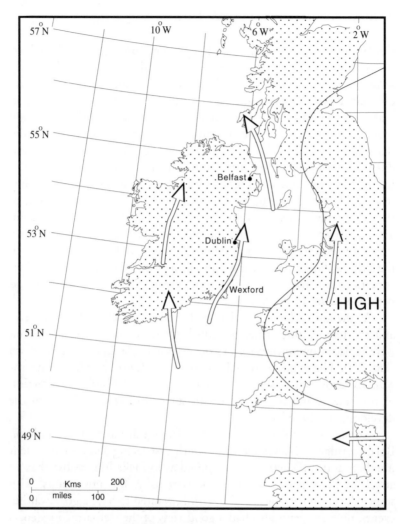

Fig 2.3. Synoptic weather map, 25 May.

light to avenge their deaths in an orgy of burning and murder. Groups of local people likewise attacked numbers of houses for arms, not a few being burned and, in some cases, the occupants killed. Flames from the now tinder-dry buildings lit up the night sky and became beacons of terror.

27 May: The Battle of Oulart Hill

On Whit Sunday, the militia and yeomanry converged on the rebels. About 2-3,000 of them chose to make a stand near Oulart Hill. They were opposed by 100 infantry, the relatively inexperienced and poorly disciplined North Cork Militia and nineteen cavalry. These troops had marched from Wexford along small country roads. Their route took them across an area of glacial sands on a road surface much sandier than most in Ireland.[14] The dry weather had made it very loose and dusty and made marching very tiring. The most direct route to Oulart for the force was about ten miles, although a sweeping movement they made to the east added up to three more. They marched in the heat of the day, having started at 11am and engaged the rebels a little after 2pm. The march was hard work and the men became tired and thirsty. They stopped at Kavanagh's pub at Ballinamonabeg, slaked their thirst with the stock of liquor and set the pub on fire. This did not improve their condition and maybe the alcohol impaired both their judgement and performance in the battle to come.

As the anticyclonic circulation drifted over Ireland from the east and the temperatures rose, the southerly winds on its western flank were replaced by northwesterlies on its eastern flank, as over Wexford (Fig. 2.4). The winds were only moderate to fresh breezes. But north-westerly air is much clearer than southerly air, and both the direction of the breezes and the clarity of the air contributed critically to the development of the battle.

Colonel Foote first saw the rebels from a distance of one mile on Bolaboy ridge.[15] They were on a south-east-facing slope in sufficient numbers and sufficiently well disposed as to make him realise that an attack by his small force would be very risky. His raw troops, with some false confidence induced by drink, wanted to have a go. Awaiting events, the insurgents also had a good view of the well-armed redcoats below them. Many rebels became terrified. They wavered and growing numbers began to flee across the top of the hill to the north. Several sources say that as they did so, they clearly saw a distant cavalry force northwards of them.[16] The cavalry were probably from Gorey. Their distance made them unaware of the battle; they neither saw nor heard anything. They heard nothing because the sound of the conflict that now developed would have carried on the wind to the southeast, not to the northwest. But the insurgents assumed their intent was to trap them, so they crowded back to their lines. From that moment they were all committed to fight, believing there was no retreat.

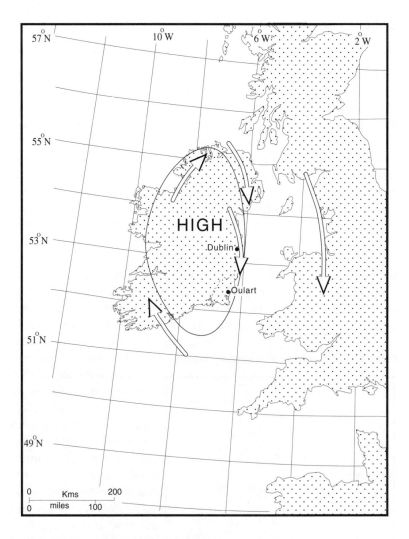

Fig 2.4. Synoptic weather map, 27 May.

Whether Colonel Foote was distracted by sending a message for reinforcements and others took the initiative, or whether it was his own strategy, is not known. His troops charged up the hill. They quickly became so breathless and unco-ordinated that they could neither move nor reload fast enough. Once the uphill charge petered out the rebels surged forward and piked most of the force to death, only five escaping back to Wexford.

28 May: The Battle of Enniscorthy

The persistent high pressure system dominating Irish weather now evolved into a complex pattern of cells. A circulation developed between Wexford and Wales that produced light, westerly winds across central and northern County Wexford, including Enniscorthy (Fig. 2.5). Although of little strength, these westerlies had a significant role in one of the most important engagements of the rebellion.[17]

Another dry, hot day developed. It became the hottest day of the month for many places in Ireland. With new confidence from the victory at Oulart, new arms from the vanquished and new recruits, the rebels converged on Enniscorthy and attacked shortly after midday. The attack began outside the Duffrey Gate and along Irish Street, on the north-western side of the town (Fig 2.6). As the defenders were forced back the tinder dry thatched houses were set on fire.[18] This spread quickly and the streets soon filled with smoke.[19] The wind pushed the smoke from Duffrey Gate, Guttke Street, Drumgold Street and Irish Street into the faces of the defenders, forcing them to retreat eastwards to Market Square. It is recorded that 'Smoke filled the streets so that yeomen could not see the rebels till they were charged by their pikes' and 'half suffocated by the smoke of the burning houses, which prevented a clear view of their opponents, they were at length forced to retire'.[20] Typical of anticyclonic conditions, the wind hardly dispersed the smoke. But the high air temperatures combined with the heat of the fires made it rise slowly from the surface, and was described as a 'pillar', 'plume' and a 'great pall of smoke' in Wexford, sixteen miles away.[21]

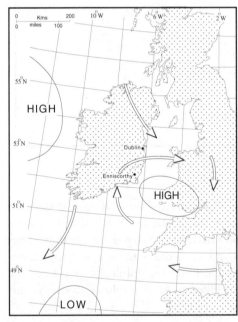

Fig 2.5. Synoptic weather map, 28 May.

The insurgents also tried to cross the River Slaney in the shallows above the town's bridge, but they were too exposed to musket fire. However, dry weather had lowered

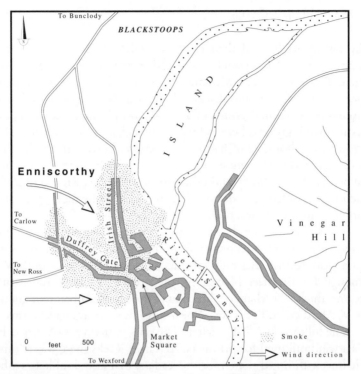

Fig 2.6. The effect of wind and smoke at Enniscorthy, 28 May.

the water level sufficiently to allow them to cross at Blackstoops.[22] Thus the Slaney's catchment must have had little rainfall for some time, in contrast to the regular showers near Dublin. Having crossed the river and being able to advance along the eastern bank, the rebels pushed the defenders back towards the bridge. After two hours the defenders abandoned the town by turning the smoke to their advantage. Using the smoke as a cover they withdrew from the bridge and escaped along the Wexford road. The rebels missed the chance of capturing their much-needed arms. But they had gained a great deal. They had seized the centre of the county and new recruits now flocked to them.

In contrast, in Dublin the master of the *Dorset* recorded rain showers during the day. As important as high temperatures producing convective uplift may have been, the synoptic map shows that over the east coast and Irish Sea air streams from the northwest and west converged. Thus, two shower-producing mechanisms, convection and convergence, combined to produce weather conditions quite different from the rest of Ireland.

29 MAY: HILLTOP CAMPS

The insurgents formed their camps on hilltops. After the victory at Enniscorthy, one was established on Vinegar Hill and the next day at Three Rocks on Forth Mountain near Wexford. Carrigrew in the north, Carrickbyrne and Lacken Hill near New Ross also became important. As natural points of assembly people streamed to them as recruits (willingly or otherwise) while others had little alternative, having lost their homes and had no protection. Thus, among the thousands who gathered there were women and children, the traumatised, the bereaved, the elderly and other non-combatants who were glad to reach relative safety. For days groups sought them by night, glad of the starlight and the dry weather.

The idyllic weather that made camp life possible was almost immediately threatened by depression from the south (Fig. 2.7). However, it was a weak feature that only introduced cloud across the south coast, although for the fleet blockading the French off Brest the weather became 'thick'.[23] It changed direction to the southeast before it got near the Wexford coast, but it was a 'near miss' in meteorological terms.

The hilltops had little shelter. The only structure on Vinegar Hill was a windmill used for prisoners. At Three Rocks there was a 'miserable hut' with holed thatch for the leaders, that also doubled as a hospital.[24] How much shelter it provided is doubtful. However, the weather on most days was similar to this day – warm and dry, so little was required, despite the hilltops being one or two degrees cooler than elsewhere. Many peasants wore hats that gave protection from the relentless sun. At night conditions varied. Some were calm, still and mild, as on this first night camp at Three Rocks.[25] But on other nights, when clouds were few, temperatures fell and people were exposed to the cold. They were above the wet valley mists that tended to form in the early morning of such nights. The traditional 'trusty' met some needs, but not all. So the houses of neighbouring gentry were stripped of their furniture, curtains, window hangings, tablecloths and carpets (as well as their food) to make tents.[26] Their livestock were driven to the hills for food and the carcasses buried because of threatened disease in the hot weather.[27] Their cellars helped to meet the growing thirst.

The weather-related strategic qualities of the hills included good visibility across the countryside. Surprisingly, this was less help to an approaching enemy. From a richly wooded, undulating countryside hills such as Vinegar Hill are indistinguishable except at close range. General Needham's militia marching on Vinegar Hill first observed it

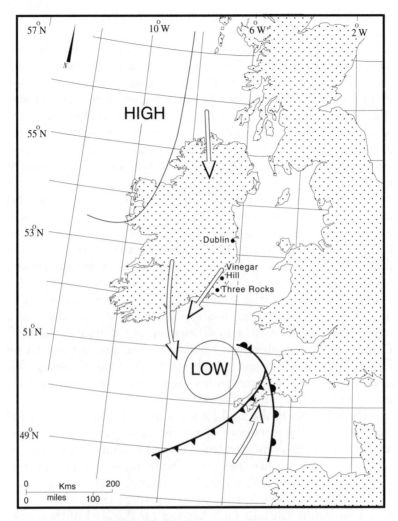

Fig 2.7. Synoptic weather map, 29 May.

when within a mile and a half.[28] To retain the insurgents as a fighting force it was essential to keep them together. The lack of rain was probably more critical than warm temperatures in making this possible and enabling the rising to continue for so long. As long as high pressure dominated the weather and blocked any approaching Atlantic depressions, this was likely to continue.

30 MAY: THE DEFENCE OF NEWTOWNMOUNTKENNEDY

Elsewhere in Ireland the rebellion had been slow to take off or had faltered badly during the first few days. County Wicklow was an important link between Wexford and Dublin.[29] To stem the tide of rebellion in the southeast required troops and equipment to pass through Wicklow. Likewise, the successful spread of the rebellion from the south to Dublin would be infinitely enhanced by the strategic capture of the garrison town of Newtownmountkennedy, the capture of its arms and the consequent isolation of Wicklow and other garrisons to the south.

Smoke again played an important part in the outcome. The rebel attack was initiated between 1am and 2am. Two rebel groups were to have attacked simultaneously from each end of the town, which was linear in form. But without waiting for the second group to arrive from the nearby coastal area, the first group advanced from the northern end of the town, set the cavalry's stables on fire and attacked the barracks.

Captain Bourganey led a defending force that consisted of a mixture of militia and cavalry. In desperate straits he decided to use a smoke screen in an attempt to disorientate and confuse the rebels.[30] Despite protests, loyalist-owned buildings were among those set on fire, including the garrison's headquarters, Armstrong's hotel. This strategy appears to have met with some success as it slowed the rebel attack, without stopping it altogether.

The behaviour of the smoke was determined entirely by the wind conditions and the turbulence of the air. Throughout the day there had been an anticyclonic circulation around Ireland centred over the northwest of the country (Fig. 2.8). The resulting winds on the east coast were light and from a northerly direction. Under the cloud cover that appears to have been widespread across the country the nighttime temperature fall was much less and the dispersal of the smoke much slower than would have occurred under cloudless skies The thickening, lingering smoke would have been much to Bourganey's satisfaction. It blunted the rebel attack and gave him the opportunity to make a desperate counter attack with his cavalry against the rebel pikemen who were threatening the magazine, which seemed to be the main target of the attack. The counter attack was expensive and despite cavalry losses, including Bourganey himself, the rebels were halted and began to withdraw just as the second group of rebels arrived. In the smoke it was difficult for them to find out what was going on and they were unable to change the tide of the battle. But they did provide some

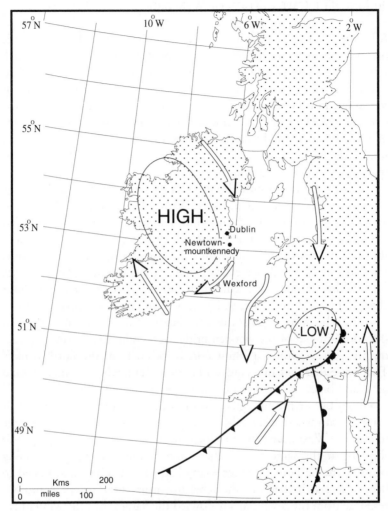

Fig 2.8. Synoptic weather map, 30 May.

cover for their fellow insurgents to withdraw.

Not only did atmospheric conditions influence this critical battle, but it appears to have been one of the very few occasions when a smoke screen was deployed by loyalist forces with deliberate intent. Often the tactical use of weather conditions appears to have been opportunistic rather than calculated, even among experienced generals.

30 May: The Capitulation of Wexford

After the rebel successes, the Protestant population in the countryside began to abandon their homes for the perceived security of Wexford. Relieved that there was no immediate attack on the town by the rebels massing outside in their camp at Three Rocks, Wexford's garrison sent to Duncannon Fort for reinforcements. It also prepared to defend the town by removing the now tinder-dry thatch house roofs at the edge of the town that might catch fire.[31] Refugees from Enniscorthy had told of the devastating effect of the fire and smoke, and no effort was spared to avoid a repetition.

However, the synoptic situation had changed sufficiently to make a repeat of that experience unlikely. With a depression over Wales and an anticyclone over Ireland, the winds had become northeasterly (Fig. 2.8). These winds were not strong but they were sufficient to hinder the spread of fire and smoke into the town from the western side. However, these winds were also fickle as the alternating land and sea breezes that frequently occurred in hot weather could bring about changes in wind direction, so it was wise to take these precautions.

The rebel move against the town began in the early morning when the northern end of the wooden bridge across the River Slaney was set on fire. An eyewitness account noted a wind from the north bank.[32] This was either part of a land-sea breeze system, which at night would be a land breeze to open water, or merely the regional northerly wind produced by the pressure gradient towards the depression (Fig 2.9). It is not certain whether the rebels were trying to use it to their advantage to trap the Wexford garrison in the town and to damage the quays and shipping at the same time – there were numerous ships and fishing boats in the harbour in which many had sought refuge and hoped to flee to Wales. If that was the rebel intention, they failed. A prompt response from the town quickly dowsed the flames. But the wind drove the fire sufficiently along the bridge to create enough damage to delay the advance of the rebels into Wexford later that day. This prevented them seizing the town before the garrison fled with its arms and artillery to Duncannon Fort – a considerable loss to the rebels, who had been hoping to gain large supplies of arms and military equipment.

The early hours of the morning also saw significant action on the slopes of Forth Mountain, in which the thick cloud cover took a hand. Part of a relief column from Duncannon Fort was surprised by rebels, largely wiped out and its artillery seized. One aspect of this event has puzzled historians. The column was following the main relief force led

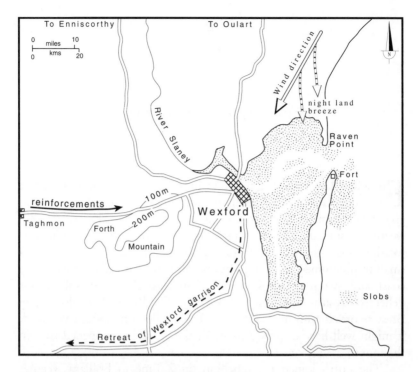

Fig 2.9. Wind and the fall of Wexford, 30 May.

by General Fawcett that had halted at Tagmahon for the night. The following column passed them by and later ran into the ambush. Had the following column met up with the main force there is little doubt that it would have stayed with them until the following morning. Then they would have advanced as one. Why this did not happen has been a puzzle to many. But the explanation for this is probably quite simple. The moonless cloudy night was probably so dark that there was no sight of the main force bivouacked in the fields away from the main routeway.[33]

This early morning victory put the rebels in good heart so that when the Wexford garrison sent out negotiators they were in no mood to compromise, attacking them and chasing them back into the town. About the same time the garrison fled to Duncannon, burning and killing as it went, and the distant trail of destruction soon became apparent from the camp on Forth Mountain as smoke and flames marked the progress of its soldiers.

3

JUNE: A GOLDEN SUMMER

For a few days at the beginning of June the weather almost broke. It was touch and go as suddenly the pressure began to fall in the north giving small amounts of rain for four days (Fig 3.1). Then sunny, dry weather resumed and the summer became truly golden. The fine weather was also attacked from the south. There, the advance of a small troublesome depression was also blocked. Instead of crossing the coast and sweeping across Cork, Waterford and Wexford, it was deflected towards Cornwall and Brittany. The British fleet blockading Brest recorded rain, mist and fog.[1] Had it fallen on County Wexford, it might well have dispersed many of the rebels, as happened later in the month.

The north joined the rebellion on 7 June in brilliant weather enjoyed by the entire country. In key battles at Antrim and Ballynahinch the wind played a significant part. The Wexford rising continued until 22 June, although the action paused as General Lake waited for reinforcements to implement his low-risk strategy based on overwhelming force.[2] The chances of its success magnified many-fold when the rebels failed to capture key border towns.

The rebellion's demise roughly coincided with the end of this 'golden summer'. Pressure systems underwent a basic change on 18 June as anticyclonic influences declined (Fig 3.1). During the month temperatures had been rising. By 17 June they had reached 24°C in Armagh, when afternoon temperatures in the southeast would have been close to 30°C. But within three days they fell by up to 10 degrees (Fig 3.3).[3] The rain was even more significant. It disrupted rebel dispositions outside New Ross and allowed British forces to advance. During a stormy weekend (21-22 June) Wexford was surrendered to the victorious Lake.

Many insurgents escaped from to neighbouring counties. The weather continued to affect their fortunes. But it was never as advantageous to them as it had been during the first month of the rising. The significant moment of opportunity it presented had passed by.

Temperature

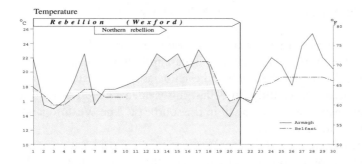

Pressure

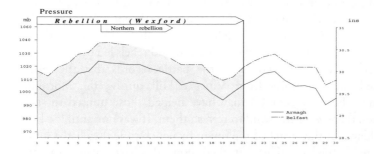

Raindays

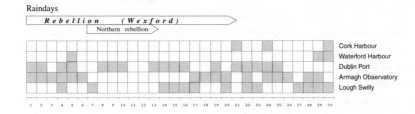

Rainfall

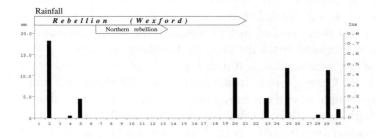

Fig 3.1. Temperature, pressure, raindays and rainfall amounts (Belfast), June 1798.

1 June: Heat, Thirst and Dust in North Wexford

After two weeks without rain a depression disturbed Ireland as far south as Dublin. In Derry, Armagh, Belfast and Dublin small amounts of rain fell during the afternoon and evening as the depression's fronts advanced across the country. In Belfast this yielded a mere 1.8mm (Fig 3.2).[4] But there was no rain at all in the southeast. The Wexford land-scape was looking very dry.

Bunclody was one of the key Wexford towns considered necessary to capture in order to gain full control of the county. However, the Crown forces considered it essential to hold on to it to block any rebel advance on Carlow and spreading the rising beyond Wexford.[5] So Colonel L'Estrange was sent to defend it with about 350 men and two guns. He arrived just ahead of several thousand rebels led by Fr Kearns.

Taylor's detailed account of the battle records that the rebels marched the ten miles from Vinegar Hill during the morning. Although the early coolness may have helped those unused to such marches, there was little wind to refresh them. It was not until the heat of midday that they reached the town, by which time they had a lot of very tired stragglers.[6] They attacked along the River Slaney to turn L'Estrange's flank. To avoid this, L'Estrange withdrew. With the town in their grasp, some rebels tried to silence the fire from loyalists defend-ing their homes, while others slaked their considerable thirst with whiskey from cellars and became intoxicated (although some historians doubt this).[7] Unprepared for L'Estrange's counter-attack, the rebels were routed, fleeing with heavy losses.

Further to the east, one of the largest rebel camps was on Carrigrew Hill, the highest ground between Oulart and Gorey. This was well-placed for an advance northwards to Arklow. As a preliminary step to this it was decided to attack the small garrison in Gorey. So about 1,000 men marched to Ballyminaun Hill, which commanded Gorey, to camp and attack the town the following morning.

But they were forestalled. A patrol spotted them and reported their move to the Gorey garrison. Its full force, about 218 militia and caval-ry, moved out to meet them during the afternoon. The numerical odds were clearly against them. As they advanced, the very dry weather made their progress something of a spectacle that was very obvious even from a distance. The high afternoon temperatures and the lack of wind resulted in clouds of dust rising from the parched roads. It was so thick and rose so high into the air that it made the rebels believe they were being confronted by a far larger force than was in fact the case.[8] So,

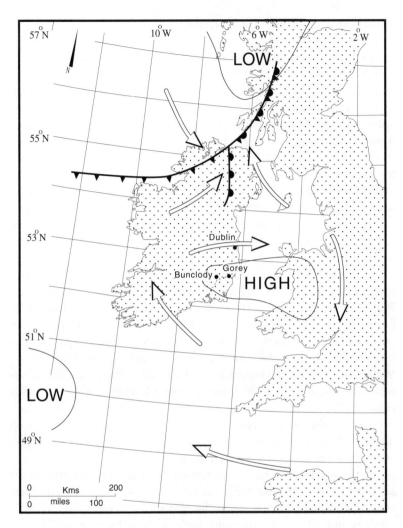

Fig 3.2. Synoptic weather map, 1 June.

when the forces met just outside Ballycanew, the rebels held back and engaged in a sustained musketry duel rather than attacking in large numbers with their pikes. This favoured the better-armed troops, and the rebels broke and fled back to Carrigrew. The army's victory gave them three precious additional days in which to bring reinforcements to Gorey.[9]

4 JUNE: AN AMBUSH AT TUBERNEERING

Tuberneering is a small steep rocky cliff overlooking the road out of Gough village in County Wexford. It is unusual because there were not many defiles like it along the roads of the county in 1798. It is hidden by a bend in the road. The rock marked a change from a relatively open to a much more wooded countryside. The trees suddenly become dense. In the bright sunlight and heavy foliage of the 1798 summer this would have been even more marked as the deep shadows cast into the defile would contrast sharply with the bright sun-filled sky facing users of the road travelling southwards. The small tongue of high pressure extending over south-east Ireland was just sufficient to keep County Wexford dry and warm, when other areas of Ireland were experiencing small amounts of rain from a depression off the north coast (Fig 3.3).

General Loftus had reinforced Gorey and decided on a two-pronged attack against the large camp at Carrigrew Hill. Colonel Walpole and 300 men, with three pieces of artillery, led the advance. Loftus advanced along a parallel route to the east. He could easily pick out Walpole by his scarlet uniform and tall grey horse. But he was also very visible to the rebels he was bent on destroying. Even before Walpole left Gorey, the insurgents had learned of the attack and decided to take the offensive. Walpole dismissed a warning that the rebels knew his intentions and even had the messenger thrown into gaol. Meanwhile, the rebels prepared an ambush, using the rock, the deep ditches behind the high banks and thick hedges bordering the road. All overlooked the defile and were adorned by a canopy of trees.[10]

Walpole advanced with a confidence not shared by his officers. As his force turned into the defile the road narrowed and their progress became slow and difficult. Then the trap was sprung. An assault with muskets and pikes from the sides took Walpole by surprise. He was killed in the first attack and a desperate containing action was fought by his men. Loftus was nearby and the sound of fighting reached him, but he did not send any reinforcements. The terrain hid the action from Loftus' view and he assumed Walpole was clearing a rebel outpost. When Loftus realised what was happening he sent a detachment of cavalry. But they were spotted, attacked and mostly wiped out. Walpole's officers saw they were being surrounded and pulled back. With Loftus' column, they retreated first to Gorey, but severely harried by the rebels, they fell back further, to Arklow.

Much of north County Wexford was now abandoned by the army

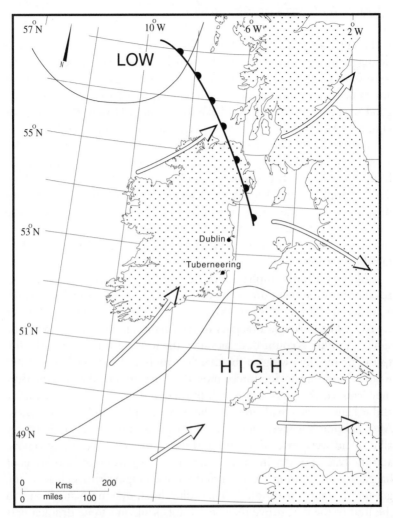

Fig 3.3. Synoptic weather map, 4 June.

as well as a large proportion of the Protestant population. The defeat halted the operation to clear north Wexford of insurgents. This was of great significance for the insurgents further south as it gave more time to organise, and raised morale to new heights. The victory was one of the few occasions when the Wexford insurgents deliberately used the natural advantages of their environment in any effective way. As a result, the rebels gained one of their most decisive victories.

5 June: The Battle of New Ross

Did it rain during the battle of New Ross? There is no account of the battle suggesting that it did. Yet all the available weather information points to this as a probability. It is certain that the combatants were unaware of any rain. But if it did occur, it dents the view that there was unbroken good weather throughout the Wexford rebellion. However, if it did not rain, then Wexford's weather was quite remarkable and exceptional.

At midday in Belfast 4.6mm of rain was recorded.[11] The observer at Armagh noted 'heavy rain' in the afternoon, while at midday in Dublin there was 'heavy showers and hail' and at nearby Waterford 'rain'.[12] South of Dublin the wind was from the southwest, but from the northwest in the northern half of the country. The rain, its nature and the veering wind all suggest that at about noon a cold front was moving to the southeast (Fig 3.4). The action at New Ross ended during the afternoon.[13]

All the accounts emphasise the heat and dryness. So, when the rebel advance into the town drove the defenders across the River Barrow, for a pocket of resisting soldiers, 'Mrs McCormick, mixed wine and water … conveying welcome draughts to men fighting under the fierce June sun'.[14] Another account describes how the town 'was in flames, the fire spreading rapidly owing to the thatched roofs and the long spell of dry weather' and that having forced most defenders to retreat across the river they 'entered the houses in search of food and drink … hungry, thirsty and exhausted they had survived the burden and heat of several hours'. After fighting 'for seven hours … in the gross heat of that June day … all of them were covered in dust and sweat, the soot of burning cabins, and the black powder from the cannon. [They] dissolved into knots of haggard men hunting for food and spirits, flinging themselves to the ground in their exhaustion'.[15] Their dire thirst, due in no small part to the heat of the day, drove their search for drink and some drunkenness that followed.[16] As a result, they were no match for General Johnson's counter-attack across the drawbridge that the rebels had failed to raise.

A few miles distant from New Ross a terrible event occurred that does provide some other evidence for a frontal passage. During the day, at Scullabogue, a thatched barn was set on fire by the rebels with about 100 prisoners inside. Dinah Goff, at Horetown House, saw the smoke of the burning barn and mentions in her account 'the strong and dreadful effluvium which was wafted from it to our lawn' three and a half miles away'.[17] Horetown House was to the southeast of Scullabogue, so the morning south-west wind had veered to the north-

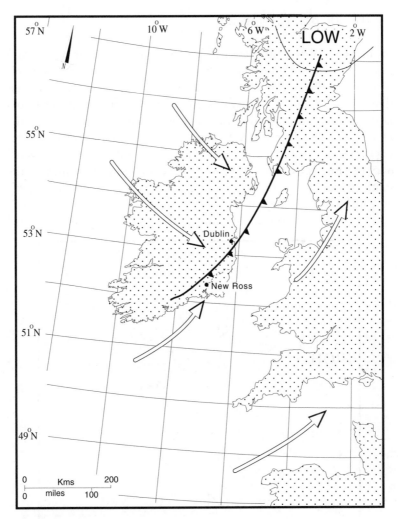

Fig 3.4. Synoptic weather map, 5 June.

west, an indication that a front had passed. But there were no reports of rain.

The front must have weakened as it reached the southeast, where it produced patchy rain at best, petering out as the descent coastwards from Blackstairs Mountains suppressed uplift. Thus, the wind still veered as the front passed, but there was little rain. If there were some light, isolated showers near New Ross, the men fighting for their lives took little notice.

7 June: The Battle of Antrim

In the north of Ireland there had been spasmodic falls of rain until 6 June. This ended significantly when two antycyclones came to dominate the weather and prevent any further intrusion of Atlantic depressions (Fig 3.5). One from the west arrived overnight, pushed cool northwesterly winds across Ulster and produced a few showers on the Donegal coast.[18] To the east, less cloud made for more effective warming so the air dried as it crossed the land. A second centre had lingered over the English Channel, but now brought southerly winds to the south coast. Pressure built rapidly during the day to herald a dry period which lasted throughout the Ulster rising.

The early mists produced by the cold and relatively calm dawn had

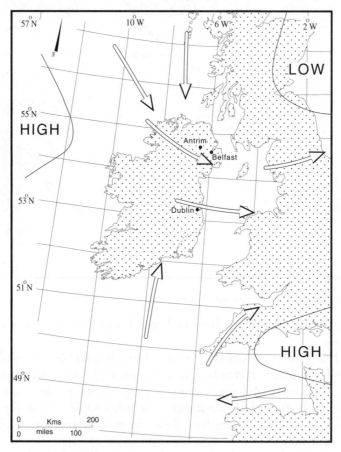

Fig 3.5. Synoptic weather map, 7 June.

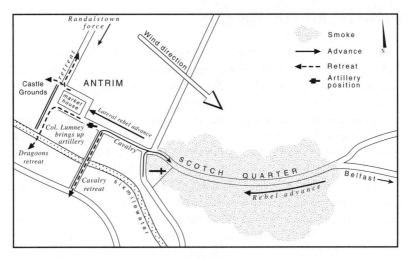

Fig 3.6. Smoke drift at the battle of Antrim.

largely disappeared by the time Henry McCracken led his men to a rendezvous on Donegore Hill above Antrim town with several thousand others.[19] In the crisp, clear, northwesterly air their view from a height of 800 feet took in Randalstown and Ballymena, from which tell-tale smoke indicated other actions were in progress.[20]

As the rebels approached Antrim, the garrison set fire to the Scotch Quarter (Fig 3.6). Dense smoke billowed from the thatch, damp from the recent rain. With a light wind and a cool day, the smoke did not disperse readily, tending to hang and drift delaying McCracken's attack (perhaps fatally) for about an hour.[21] About 2.30pm, he advanced. But by this time reinforcements under Colonel Lumney arrived with two curricle guns. Entering the town from the south between the advancing rebels and the market square, the guns were directed along the street at the rebels, but with little effect because the dense smoke obscured their target.[22] For a while the smoke gave a marked advantage to the rebels. Lumney therefore decided to use his cavalry. But their charge was from clear air into the dense smoke and ended in confusion and severe losses. The rebels pressed home their attack into the breeze and clearer air but this made them easier targets and their own losses began to rise. Then arriving rebel reinforcements from Randalstown mistook retreating defenders as a sortie from a victorious garrison. They panicked and scattered when they could have carried the day. The panic spread to McCracken's men, who wavered and began to desert when a force led by Colonel Durham arrived.[23] McCracken saw that the day was lost and retreated into the Slemish Mountains.

9 June: The Battle of Saintfield

There was little change to the strong high pressure system that sat over Ireland and produced one of the highest pressure observations of the summer (Fig 3.1). Across Ulster the winds were still light and from the northwest, while temperatures were rising only slowly (Fig 3.7).

The United Irishmen of County Down prepared to make their move. Late on 8 June a large number gathered on Ouley Hill two miles from Saintfield. The following morning a group of them attacked the home of loyalist Hugh McKee and burnt it out, with all its occupants. In response to this atrocity, Colonel Stapleton was sent with 300 men and two pieces of artillery from Newtownards. The insurgents knew of their approach and prepared an ambush. They deployed their forces, probably several thousand strong, to maximise the advantages of the local drumlin terrain of small hills and marshy hollows. On a hillside just outside Saintfield, hedges and ditches bordered the road behind which musketeers were placed. These were overlooked by partially-wooded high ground of the Price estate, where pikemen were placed. Below the road was a stretch of wet, marshy ground that would limit the deployment of the troops once they had entered the ambush as well as an extent of woodland where other pikemen were placed. The summer foliage on the trees and in the undergrowth was very dense, providing ample cover on all sides.

It was probably about 5pm when Stapleton halted about half a mile from Saintfield to reconnoitre. Two volunteers rode down the road to the town but failed to see the rebels behind the hedges and trees. With great control the rebels allowed both to return to Stapleton, who then ordered the advance. Then the self-control broke. As Stapleton's force entered the trap, the desire for revenge for past wrongs was so strong that a United Irishman opened fire. His target fell, but the trap was sprung. At almost point blank range the insurgents fired and there was a temporary panic. The cavalry, crowded by the terrain, was badly hit. An attempt to seize the guns was parried and the guns turned on the attackers, forcing them back. Stapleton seized the opportunity for a strategic retreat. A stand-off ensued until dusk when, leaving many dead and wounded, Stapleton retired to Comber. This was the only success by the rebels in Ulster against regular troops.

A curious question arises as to why the reconnaissance failed to spot the rebels. The weather may well have played a part. It was a particularly bright sunny day.[24] Stapleton arrived from the northeast and

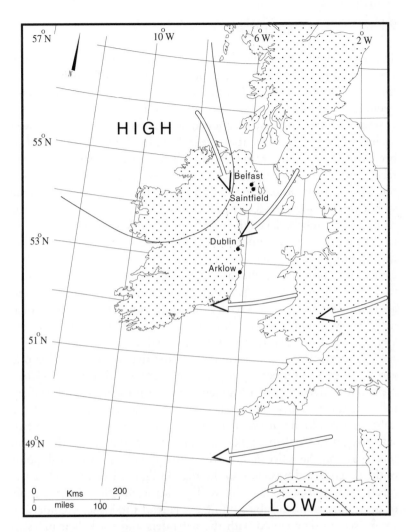

Fig 3.7. Synoptic weather map, 9 June.

his force was facing directly into the afternoon sun. From the hill over Saintfield the sky was very open. In these conditions shadows within woodland appear dense and dark.[25] On the lower side of the road the shadows would have been towards the two who carried out the reconnaissance and they would have been growing at this time of day. The sheer brightness of the weather may have dulled their vision and led them into a fatal ambush.

9 June: The Battle of Arklow

The anticyclonic winds over Ireland were circulating in their typical clockwise direction (Fig 3.7). At times they were so light that conditions were almost calm, and in the absence of any wind the high temperatures seemed even hotter, particularly to men on the march.

So, another hot day developed as the Wexford rebels moved against Arklow to open the route to Dublin. In Dublin Castle, this had been feared and reinforcements were being rushed there. From the rebel camp near Gorey the march should have taken about three hours, but it took many more. There were several delays. The weather became so hot that frequent rests were made. At Coolgreany some historians report that numbers slaked their thirst with whiskey and became intoxicated, although this cannot have affected very many.[26] But during these hours of delay a major strategic advantage was lost.[27] A few days earlier the military had abandoned Arklow. Now they were rushing back, arriving every hour. At 1pm the Durham Regiment arrived, and an hour later the Gorey Cavalry came in from Dublin. Additional defences were thrown up until 3pm when an outpost informed General Needham that the rebels were in sight.[28]

The battle began about 4pm and lasted five to six hours. Despite vastly superior numbers the pikemen were disadvantaged against Needham's firepower, even though the rebel musketeers and artillery inflicted severe losses. Although the action was very severe and the fighting very bloody in the main frontal attack on the town, the two sides fought to a stalemate. Perhaps the most critical part of the action took place on the rebel right, at the Fishery. This was the weak point of the defence and was close to the road bridge to Dublin.[29] Here the rebels made considerable progress. They set fire to the thatched roofs of the empty wooden cabins lining the lane of the Fishery. Under the smoke screen they closed with the defenders and used their pikes to extreme effect.[30] They also successfully repulsed a counter-attack by some of Needham's cavalry. It is probable that a light inland afternoon sea breeze drifted the smoke slowly across the road and trapped it in the lane (Fig 3.8). The breeze was weak so the smoke thickened and was probably responsible for 'friendly fire' deaths among the defenders.[31] Only a gap in the buildings prevented the flames reaching the rest of the town. With this encouragement the rebels centre and left vigorously renewed their own attack. Needham's nerve almost failed him and he contemplated a retreat across the bridge.[32] But about 8pm the breeze weakened and backed as the land cooled and

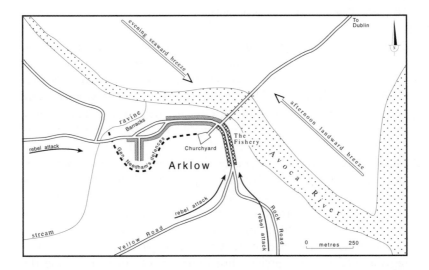

Fig 3.8. The changing wind direction at the battle of Arklow.

downslope katabatic winds along the valley of the River Avoca began to roll the smoke southwards into the face of the rebels. Later it would back further and flow seawards. The initial benefit of the smoke screen had been reversed.[33] So dramatic was this change that the defenders reckoned 'that the wind at the order of our God, turned, drove it from us and confounded them in their own device'.[34] Semi-blinded and in disarray, the rebels were pushed back along the coast road. With little ammunition left, and fading light, they withdrew, conceding the day.

The rebels retreated for the night to Gorey Hill, a few miles to the south. Many hundreds (possibly more than 1,000) had been killed and several hundred wounded. Fortunately for them Needham did not order order his cavalry to pursue the retreating insurgents. Otherwise the number of fatalities would have been much higher. This was because the density of ditches and hedges were considered too much of a hazard and the cavalry had received a severe blow to its morale in the reverse it suffered at the Fishery.

The failure at Arklow allowed Lake to advance his policy of encirclement of County Wexford to be followed, by compressing rebel forces into its centre where they could be attacked with maximum force. Lake's new offensive was about to begin.

10 June: Portaferry Abandoned

The visibility remained excellent while the high pressure centre stayed in the north and pushed air southwards across Ireland (Fig 3.9). The air was cooler than if the anticyclone had been in a position over Britain. Then Ireland would have been in the path of warmer, more moist air, typically tending to a greater haziness, streaming in from a southern direction. The clear visibility helped both sides at Portaferry.

Windmill Hill overlooks Portaferry, at the tip of the Ards peninsula. It commands a view that extends many miles, especially when the air is clear.[35] From early morning Captain Matthews, the local commander, posted a lookout on the hill to warn of any rebel approach. He knew the United Irishmen in the area were strong and had recently received arms and he doubted that his force could resist a sustained attack. Prudently, he had made defensive preparations by partly closing the market house arches with improvised walls and making the building relatively fireproof. There he planned to make a stand if attacked. Southwards from Windmill Hill the view was across the narrow opening to Strangford Lough – his only escape route. Although a revenue cutter was anchored off the quay, retreating in that direction while under attack would be extremely hazardous. Even though the wind was northeasterly, it was extremely slack, and would make the vessel extremely vulnerable.

On other hills away from the town the insurgents were also watching. Although lacking telescopic aids, the air was so clear they saw that no reinforcements had arrived to aid the small yeomanry garrison in the town. This was their opportunity to take the town and also cross the straits to link with the Downpatrick rebels. Large numbers poured down the hillsides and soon appeared in the confined narrow streets of the town. They advanced with the high expectation of seizing the entrance to the Lough. But Matthews was ready. As he directed musket fire on the insurgents, the revenue cutter's cannon, with considerable accuracy only possible when the water is relatively smooth (as when the wind is from the northeast) also fired into the narrow streets into which the rebels surged. They wavered as numbers were cut down and then retreated in the face of the onslaught. Having deterred the rebel advance once, but fearing another attack that would overwhelm his force by sheer numbers, Matthews seized the opportunity of evacuating his men across the straits to Strangford. These were anxious hours. The retreat was as slow as Matthews had expected, the light breezes prolonging the operation for what seemed an eternity.

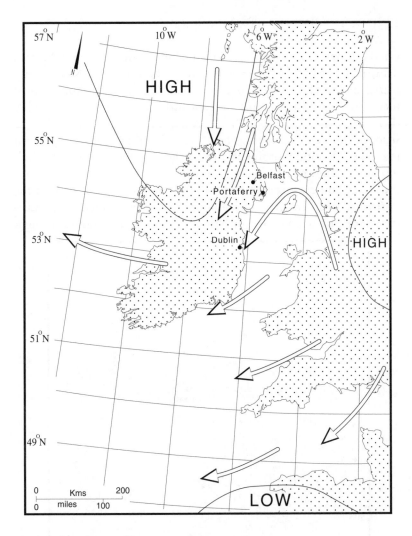

Fig 3.9. Synoptic weather map, 10 June.

Unknown to him, instead of reforming, the insurgents had retreated to Inishargie and established a camp. So Portaferry had been abandoned by both sides and neither side appear to have felt they had gained an advantage. By nightfall all of the Ards Peninsula and North Down had been abandoned to the insurgents.

45

13 June: The Battle of Ballynahinch

On 11 June Henry Munroe formed a rebel camp on Lord Moira's demesne at Ballynahinch. For two days the camp grew as the sun blazed and midday temperatures passed 20^0C.[36] Camp visitors write of men 'stretched listlessly on the green turf ...; a considerable number sheltering themselves from the scorching rays of the sun under the shade of the trees'.[37] 'Cousin Shaw and I visited the rebel camp ... on that most beautiful morning in June as the sun climbed above the hilltops and the mist lifted like a great white sheet in the valley'.[38] Thus the anticyclonic weather continued. For several days the wind in the north had been easterly. Drifting across the sea it picked up sufficient moisture to condense into shallow early morning mists as night

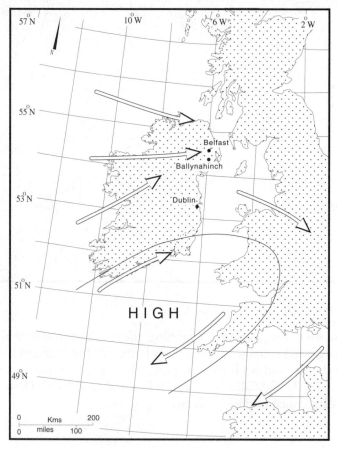

Fig 3.10. Synoptic weather map, 13 June.

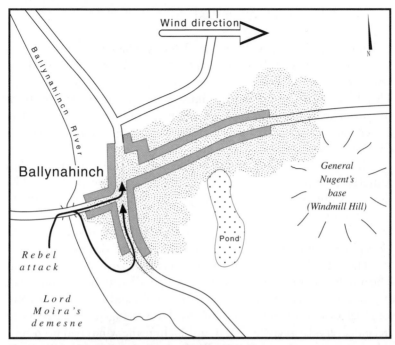

Fig 3.11. Smoke drift at the battle of Ballynahinch.

temperatures fell. But on the 12 June the anticyclone moved southwards and the barometer at Armagh fell (Fig 3.10).[39] Westerly winds now spread over Ireland and, in the late afternoon, the sun disappeared early as it slipped behind a layer of cloud advancing from the west.

General Nugent's force arrived exhausted after their march from Belfast in the searing heat of the previous day.[40] There was no mist that night. The cloud prevented the temperature falling as much as previous nights. Munroe refused a night attack despite Nugent's troops being largely disabled by exhaustion, looting or drunkenness. Disputes like this led to many leaving (now possible without blundering through mists), for the mountain refuges in the south.

At dawn, Munroe's pikemen attacked the town from the southwest and began to drive back Nugent's troops (Fig 3.11). But the battle was lost to the insurgents when they became confused. The westerly wind blew the smoke from burning buildings into the faces of Nugent's retreating men and frustrated a cavalry charge. At this point the rebels seemed poised for victory. But enveloped in smoke, the rebels mistook Nugent's bugle signal to retreat for the arrival of fresh forces.[41] As a result, after two hours of heavy fighting, the rebels started a retreat that became a rout.

16 JUNE: REINFORCEMENTS AT LAST

In Dublin Castle, viceroy Lord Camden was agitated. His priority was to ensure the safety of the capital. When the rebellion began he did not want troops deployed at the expense of the capital's security. Therefore, an offensive strategy must wait on reinforcements from Britain. The military setbacks in Wexford confirmed his view. The Ulster rising compounded the situation, but no new troops were needed there as that had been anticipated.

In Britain it was not considered necessary to commit new troops to Ireland. Those already there had suffered next to no casualties. The rising was not taken urgently until 'genteel' refugees began arriving at western ports. In early June the first of several urgent requests for large reinforcements came from the anxious Camden. Eventually this led to his replacement by Lord Cornwallis who was sent with more troops.

The delay in their arrival has been blamed partly on the weather. The problem was that the weather was so 'good', with little or no wind. It was not unusual for sailing between Britain and Ireland to involve long delays due to the wind. But to those facing the insurgents in Ireland, every day seemed vital. Until 11 June the winds had been suitable for crossing the Irish Sea. The logbook entries of the *Dorset* in Dublin port and the *Actaeon* in Liverpool show this, as well as the broader synoptic pattern. Had there been a rapid response to Camden's request, reinforcements from Britain would have sped across the Irish Sea up to 11 June, enjoying a favourable easterly wind from Liverpool. But thereafter, a high pressure system with slack variable winds dominated the southern half of the Irish Sea (compare Figs 3.10 and 3.12). The delay in sailing between 12-15 June was due mostly to light westerly winds along the northern edge of the Irish Sea anticyclone. On 15 June a fugitive from Ballynahinch, Charles Teeling, described the view from the top of Sleive Donard in County Down: 'The sun was sometime risen before I resumed my route, for I had tarried a moment to gaze on a scene the most splendid and imposing in nature. The morning was calm and serene – not a cloud obscured the sky – and the burnished sea beneath … was undisturbed by the slightest agitation on its waters.'[42] Later, 'the day was unsupportably hot, but we were often obliged to retire to the centres of the mountain from the scorching rays of the sun.'

It was not until 16 June that this pattern changed. Then the anticyclone drifted northwards and placed the middle of the Irish Sea on the southern edge of the anticyclone, changing the wind direction to

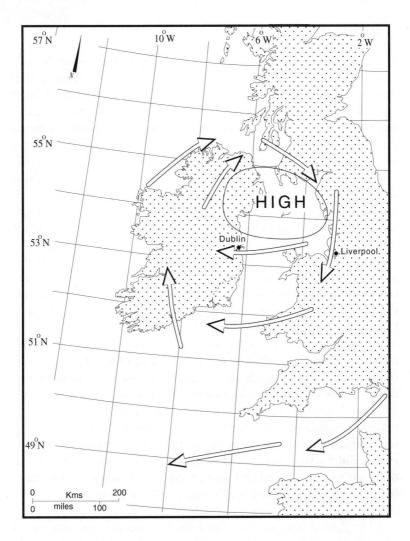

Fig 3.12. Synoptic weather map, 16 June.

north easterly and easterly (Fig 3.12). As well as being in a favourable direction the winds became stronger towards the Irish coast. On the evening of 16 June the reinforcements arrived suddenly in Dublin Bay. An additional 1,000 troops disembarked. Having been delayed by both adverse direction as well as the lightness of the wind, Lake wanted no further delay in bringing the rebellion to a speedy conclusion.

17 June: A Smoke Signal from Tinahely

Now reinforced, Lake began his move southwards. But the rebels again made an impact that suggested the campaign would not be easy. After their setback at Arklow many had moved to a camp near Mount Pleasant outside Tinahely, a noted loyalist town. In response, the garrison emerged from the town and took up defensive positions facing them. They had no real expectation of an attack. But in the early hours of the morning they found they were mistaken. The encounter was brief. The yeomen soon pulled back towards the town, then, realising they were severely outnumbered, they fled. The ease with which the rebels dispersed Tinahely's garrison and took the town was a great surprise, and a huge boost to their morale. Triumphantly they set fire to the thatched roofs and columns of smoke rose into the clear morning sky.

The anticyclone over Ireland was weakening and retreating northwards. A new anticyclone advancing from the south was still far away (Fig 3.13). Where the two air streams converged over Ulster dramatic thunderstorms developed, as at Armagh. But the winds were still only light over County Wexford. There the air warmed quickly during the morning of another sunny day, and became very unstable. As a result the smoke from Tinahely rose quickly upwards rather than spreading out as a low level haze that would have been almost invisible from a distance. The tall columns became visible for miles around above the Wicklow foothills.[43] Among those hills were insurgent bands waiting nervously to hear of events further afield. It did not take them long to realise that the town had been put to the torch; the smoke was clear evidence of the fact. As it was a loyalist town, this could mean only one thing – it had been taken by fellow-insurgents. This was the best news for some time and as renewed hope grew, many came out of their refuges and made their way to join the victors.

The fleeing yeomen met Lord Roden's cavalry. But instead of mounting a counter-attack, they all retreated to Tullow, no doubt encouraged by graphic reports from the yeomen and the tell-tale smoke, as well as their orders to avoid any engagement where the outcome was uncertain. The loss of Tinahely was setback enough without risking a more comprehensive reverse against an enemy of unknown size and capability.

Buoyant after this success, the insurgents felt more confident not only of holding off the enemy but of repeating their success if they could draw other garrisons into the open. Strong rumours of an imminent French invasion meant that a number of carefully selected victories of

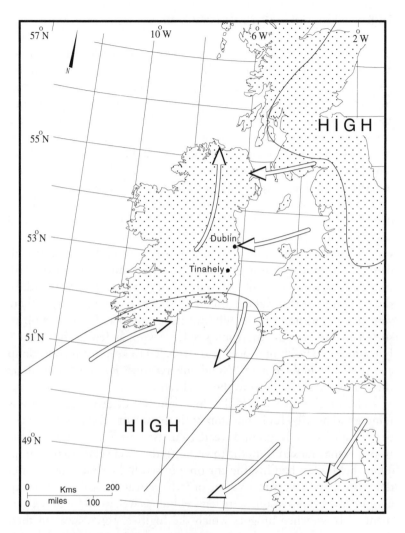

Fig 3.13. Synoptic weather map, 17 June.

this kind might keep the enemy at bay until the French arrived. The next day they marched to Kilcavan Hill as it was more suitable for defending the northwestern route into County Wexford against Lake. But this new strategy was frustrated on being ordered to Vinegar Hill where the insurgents were massing to meet Lake's advance.

19 June: The Advance from New Ross

In Ulster the weather had changed. The end of settled, dry weather came with thunder and rain on the night of 17 June, the first rain for eleven days.[44] As the high pressure collapsed and the anticyclone retreated over mainland Europe, Atlantic depressions were no longer blocked and could track across Ireland (Fig 3.14). On the morning of 19 June Armagh recorded its lowest pressure since 16 May, as a depression crossed Ireland and brought a series of fronts and their associated belts of rain.[45] In Belfast 9.8mm of rain was recorded.[46] But the account of events in County Wexford suggest that the total may have been greater there.

On 18 June at New Ross, Johnson and Major-General Moore combined forces in order to advance the next day at the same time as Lake advanced from the north. Moore's diary notes that 'The march was ordered for 2am, but from rain it was necessarily postponed till 6am'.[47] A formidable insurgent force was still camped on Lacken Hill outside New Ross. The hill had to be taken to advance on Wexford. In the event the weather did the job. When the rain came that night there was little protection on the hill and large numbers left the camp to shelter in the surrounding countryside, leaving as few as 400 men.[48] For some time Fr Philip Roche had struggled to keep the men in camp and probably doubted many would now return.[49] For this reason alone the rain was a severe blow to the rebel cause.

The attack on Lacken Hill at first light was delayed because it was raining too heavily. It did not stop until about 8am. Even then, the saturated air close to the ground created a dense mist.[50] This obscured the troops as they moved from the town, until they were close to the camp. The rebel leaders had insufficient time to recall their men, but a brief defensive ploy gave time for an orderly retreat. Large quantities of equipment and provisions were left behind, as well as 'old tattered garments and wretched brogues which the fugitives threw away in their flight, many broken bottles also; ... some stained with wine, and a little whiskey diluted with rain'.[51]

The rain spread slowly across the entire county. In the afternoon it arrived in the north as the rebels withdrew to Vinegar Hill. Gorey was reoccupied by loyalist troops as the rain arrived as a deluge forcing them to shelter.[52]

The rain has been given a significance beyond its strategic and operational importance. It was 'an ominous development at a critical time' and 'one of the most extraordinary coincidences of the summer' and 'considering the significance some of the rebels had attached to the

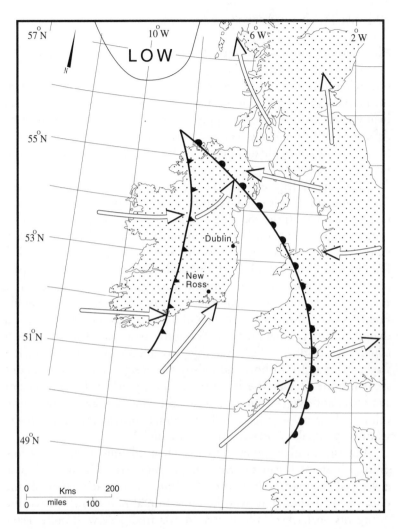

Fig 3.14. Synoptic weather map, 19 June.

spell of unbroken weather, it boded ill for their cause'.[53]

In Dublin, the departure of Camden was (appropriately) a washout. His administration of Ireland had been a failure and few were sad to see him go. The *Belfast Newsletter* recorded 'Earl Camden having been prevented by the fall of rain on Tuesday from personally paying a departing compliment to the yeomanry of this city and vicinity, has written a circular letter'.[54]

20 June: The Navy Arrives

Although the navy had been off the coast of Wexford for some days, the visibility out at sea had been very poor and it is unlikely that anyone in Wexford town had seen its ships. The town is several miles from the harbour's entrance, so it was never easy to see ships outside the bay in any case. No early warning appears to have been sent to the town by fishermen or others living along the coast who would have had a better chance of seeing them when the haze lifted and the visibility dramatically improved.[55]

A group of frigates, namely the *Endymion, Glenmore, Phoenix, Melampus* and *Unicorn*, sailed from Falmouth on 31 May and had taken up station off the coast on 2 June. They were just too late to prevent the capture of Lord Kingsborough, the commander of the North Cork Militia, on his way to join his men in Wexford. He had left Dublin, travelled by road to Arklow and sailed to Wexford to by-pass rebel-held territory, not expecting the town to be in rebel hands. The task of the frigates was to control the coastal waters and oppose the French should they arrive. For decades afterwards the rebels believed that they had commanded the Wexford coast and that the French could have landed there.[56] But this was not so. At first the frigates stayed many miles offshore and mostly out of sight. As already demonstrated, from 12 June the sea area was mostly under the influence of successive anticylones that produced light winds or calms. The warm, calm air became very hazy and at times it turned into thick foggy weather, particularly between the 12-14 June.[57]

But the weather along the coast changed fundamentally as low pressure systems began to arrive in the southeast. The first of these enveloped the frigates at 4am on 19 June, when a few miles off the Great Saltee Island. This was the same frontal rain that dispersed the insurgents on Lacken Hill. It arrived as a fresh gale with quite heavy downpours. It cleared during the morning as the wind veered to the northwest, introducing clear weather and good drying conditions in the fresh breezes that followed (Fig 3.15). At this point the ships were probably seen by the rebels on land for the first time.[58]

Lake was co-ordinating both land and sea operations. The frigates were to take control of the harbour on 20 June and neutralise the 40-50 small armed vessels there.[59] That morning, the frigates moved to the harbour entrance although it was too shallow to enter.[60] The wind, being quite fresh and blowing seaward, created problems. At one stage it seemed it would help many rebels' craft sail across the broad shallow

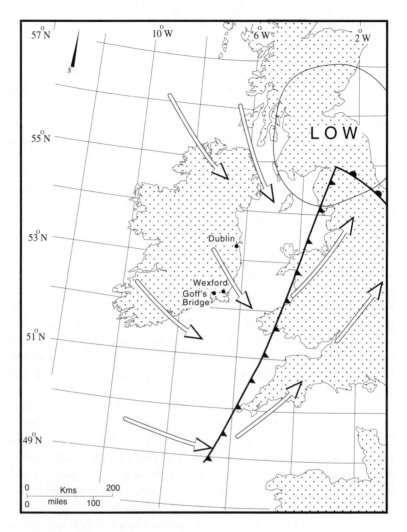

Fig 3.15. Synoptic weather map, 20 June.

harbour waters and disperse. But they were slow to recognise the opportunity and it was countered by the frigates sending four small armed
cutters into the inner harbour to fire intimidating shots towards the
quays. This action stopped them sailing, the rebels not realising they had
the wind advantage and that most of them could escape as there were
only four cutters. So they stayed and missed their opportunity.

20 June: The Battle at Goff's Bridge

Behind the rain came a sudden drop of temperature as air from the northwest invaded Ireland (Fig 3.15). Over two days the temperatures had fallen by nearly 10°C.[61] It was still warm but the intense heat had disappeared. The fresh breezes and fine weather that also followed the rain quickly dried out the lower-lying countryside. In Wexford the soils were light textured and dried quickly, so all traces of the rain soon disappeared.[62]

The speed of the rebels' retreat put Moore's advance ahead of schedule, so he swept southwards to Foulkesmills, leaving his fellow generals to head for Enniscorthy the following day. His diary records, 'The country through which we had passed was rich and beautiful, but perfectly deserted ... It was shocking to see a fine cultivated country deserted ... and in flames'.[63] During the night Fr Roche, Thomas Cloney and John Colclough gathered several thousand pikemen and several hundred with muskets from Three Rocks to halt Moore's advance. Moore first saw them about 3pm as a thick cloud of dust rising over the landscape, as they pounded over the dried out roads.[64] His early sighting gave him ample time to select strong positions west of Goff's Bridge (Fig 3.16).[65] But Moore soon realised he was outnumbered by about six to one and he alone stood between the rebels and New Ross.[66]

Because Moore had the superior firepower and the insurgents were predominantly pikemen, it was necessary for the insurgents to get to close quarters if their greater numbers and their pikes were to be used to advantage. So Roche placed his gunmen to hold the bridge against Moore while his pikemen led a series of flanking moves to the north (Fig 3.16). Had these moves outflanked Moore's left, it is possible that a famous and significant victory might have been won.

The failure of a flanking attack against Moore's left was decisive. Thomas Cloney, a rebel leader, has left a description of the battle that records the problem of dense lingering smoke that spread slowly, hampered the co-ordination of the attack and neutralised their numerical superiority: 'the fighting was in fields and woodland and along the little roadways to the west and north of the bridge ... unable to learn in which direction Father Roche had gone ... through the dense smoke which spread slowly over the battlefield ... With these [men with muskets] and a strong body of pikemen I resolved to make my way, if possible, to the main body at all hazards. The adjacent fields were now covered with a dense smoke, so as that no object was perceptible to us

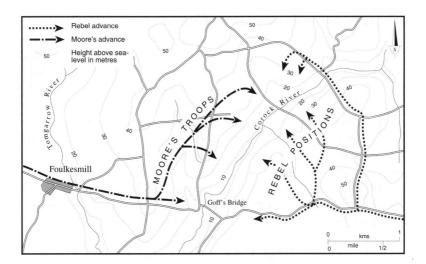

Fig 3.16. The battle of Goff's Bridge.

on the south side [where the battle was raging] at the distance of about 100 yards, nor could we conjecture what were the relative positions occupied by the contending parties ... obliged to retreat and advance in another direction ... the smoke was so thick, that it intercepted our view of the enemy until we came within a few perches of them ... with much difficulty we advanced towards and joined the main party'.[67]

The winds were light and northwesterly and the action took place in a sheltered, shallow south-facing valley, which would have made them lighter still. Smoke does not disperse readily under such conditions. It became increasingly more dense over the four to five hours of the battle and clearly caused some confusion among the rebels. But it also disguised the fact that at one stage Moore's men were faltering and a timely thrust might have won the day.[68] But the rebels were unaware that only a timely intervention by Moore himself prevented his left flank from collapsing. The dense smoke had cancelled out the advantage of using massed pikes at close quarters, particularly in the woodlands that covered some of the valley slopes and into which the battle spread. Instead, it was sufficient to tip the scales away from the rebels and at about 8pm they retreated.

21 JUNE: THE BATTLE OF VINEGAR HILL

A low pressure system moving across Scotland was followed by a ridge of high pressure from the Atlantic. Ireland lay in between. As a result, pressure was gradually rising in northern Ireland. Except for the Dublin-Wexford region, north to northwesterly winds covered Ireland and the lower temperatures brought by this air the previous day persisted (Fig 3.17). In this squally, unstable airstream there were many outbreaks of rain, some of them very heavy (as in Dublin). But the relatively sheltered county of Wexford remained dry. As a result, the distant rumbling of guns was heard distinctly in Wexford town as fifteen miles further to the north the battle for Vinegar Hill was fought, adding to the panic that swept the town that day.[69]

Any advantage accruing from the weather was to Lake's benefit. His men were able to get a little rest in the open during a series of exhausting forced marches on dry, dusty roads. Many had marched from Dublin in four days. With Johnson's force from the west and Needham's from Arklow, there were 10,000 troops, twenty artillery pieces and 400 coaches of equipment and ammunition. The rain of 19 June had ensured that the roads had not all been dust and dirt. But that had improved marching conditions only for a brief time. The journey had severely fatigued most troops, being unused to the conditions. That night they were glad to snatch a rest.

Lake's forces were at their most vulnerable the night before the battle. It was cloudy and the night was dark. Miles Byrne recalled that in the clear air thousands of fires could be seen around the hill where the insurgents gathered.[70] This was a moment of opportunity that some of the rebel leaders recognised. Little had been done to make Vinegar Hill defendable. During the day, in good visibility, the 20,000 rebels on the hill were easy targets to bombardment and musket fire, while the cavalry had open ground on the eastern side. Cloney was of the view that 'had a proposal been acceded to which was made on Vinegar Hill the evening before the battle by some of the leaders to pour down on Lake's army at Solsborough, where in consequence of extraordinary fatigue, by forced marches, they lay prostrate on the ground and unable to offer any formidable resistance, they would certainly have defeated the General, for several officers who were there with General Lake assured me, if they had been attacked that night from Vinegar Hill, they must have been inevitably destroyed'.[71]

But the opportunity was missed. Instead, after careful surveillance (for the visibility was excellent for noting the deployment details), and

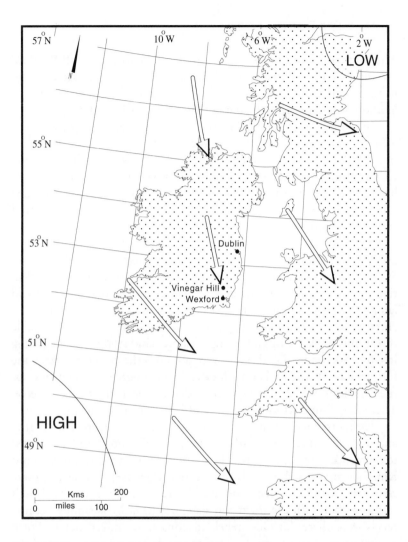

Fig 3.17. Synoptic weather map, 21 June.

with troops refreshed after their night's rest, Lake began a bombardment at about 7am. His troops and cavalry were then able to deploy almost at will. After a short resistance of two hours the rebels broke and fled southwards, where Needham had failed to complete the encirclement of the hill and town. A few miles to the west, across the River Slaney, Johnson's attack on Enniscorthy had been fiercely resisted. But there the rebels also broke and fled, joining the flight towards Wexford.

59

21 June: The Fall of Wexford

The weather had lost its heat. The captain of the *Melampus* off Wexford specifically (and unusually) noted that the wind was cold, even though it was merely a moderate breeze.[72] All over Ireland, cold air from high latitudes was depressing the temperatures (Figs 3.17 and 3.1).

In the unaccustomed coldness of the morning, Wexford's citizens were very aware that the fateful battle at Vinegar Hill had begun. The noise of Lake's bombardment carried to the town on the northerly winds, adding to the fear that gripped the town (Fig 3.18). It may have been heard also by the frigates entering the bay. Their logs recorded north-north-west winds, just the right direction for sound to travel from Enniscorthy. [73]

The four cutters needed help to neutralise the boats in the harbour, so two sloops were sent in support, the *Chapman* and the *Weazle*. With shallower draughts they could come inshore and give more effective protection than the frigates. It was intended that these should launch an attack both on the harbour and on the ruined fort at its entrance where a cannon firing on the ships posed a considerable threat. But the low tide and strong offshore wind stopped them getting in close. So, many of their crew were put onto the cutters to attack the fort, which was then taken with ease. Their progress to the quays was then made much more simple by a developing landward sea breeze. There they found Moore's troops had just entered the town.

Earlier that day, as they heard the bombardment from Enniscorthy and saw the action at the harbour entrance, Wexford's leaders decided to surrender the town to their most important captive, Lord Kingsborough. As thousands of defeated rebels began to arrive, there were fears for the loyalist prisoners. There were also fears that Lake's troops would burn the town and slaughter its citizens simply because rebels were there. So most rebels in arms were moved out to Forth Mountain or went eastwards across the river. Envoys were sent to Lake to tell him of the surrender. But they were neither seen by Lake nor given any immediate reply. At dawn the next day, word came that he would not give terms to any rebels in arms and if any prisoners were harmed the town would be annihilated. Lake still desired a military victory and there remained a dreadful prospect of death and destruction being inflicted upon the town.

If this was his intention, it was frustrated by Kingsborough and Moore. After the battle at Goff's Bridge, Moore had marched for Wexford to prevent wholesale slaughter in the town before Lake's

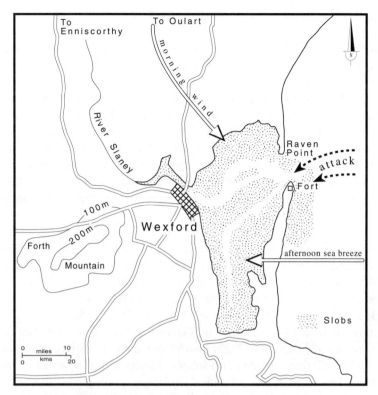

Fig 3.18. The attack on Wexford harbour.

troops arrived. He arrived as rebels were streaming into it, but he camped outside to minimise the likely excesses of his own troops. A small detachment was sent into the town and to the quays. Their sudden arrival was unexpected and caused panic. They arrived as the marines also reached the quays. These moves protected the loyalists and allowed Lake to take the formal surrender the next day. Under these circumstances Lake had little choice but to respect the surrender.

22 June: The Great Trek to County Carlow

When the morning came the weather was dry, but persistent cloud held back the temperatures. Accounts of the heat of this day that some historians have given appear to be rather exaggerated. Many seem to depend on Cloney's narrative of his forced walk back to Wexford with Lake's army.[74] As a result he learnt at first hand the hardships of a long march without a horse (it had been taken from him), during the warmest part of the day and along a rough dusty road that was stirred up by horses and carriages.[75] The campaign may have toughened him, but he still complained of the discomfort. In fact northerly winds flowing round high pressure in the west were bringing relatively cool air southwards (Fig 3.19).

Many rebels that left Wexford on 21 June ended that day in a camp at Sleedagh, south of Johnstown. Most had fought at Vinegar Hill, fled fifteen miles to Wexford, then struggled eight miles to Forth Mountain before turning southwards to their camp. They were exhausted. This was hardly ideal preparation for undertaking a remarkable trek across the county into County Carlow. But drawing on immense reserves of stamina and determination this is what they did. It is estimated that some 2,000 men set out at dawn, with their wounded, their destitute women and supply wagons along the small county roads. For many it was a familiar landscape, passing Moyglass across the moor of Mulrankin to Goff's Bridge and on to Killan. Then using the old road close to Knockroe they passed through the Scullogue Gap into County Carlow.

During the afternoon winds swirling around a depression in the Celtic Sea brought increasing amounts of cloud from the north, moderating the temperatures. This would have been a great relief as they struggled across country, trying to conserve their energy and avoid dehydration. The cool wind blowing in their faces as they headed northwards would have made their exertions much more endurable than if the sun had been blazing down. In all, the weather could not have been more kind.

The barracks at Killedmund was their first military obstacle. They approached it across the bogs to cut off the garrison's escape route through the Crumlin Gap, and then successfully attacked them with pikes. The barrack was burned down, rendering it useless for guarding the gap. Only then did they camp for the night. Their camp was four miles inside County Carlow, so they had covered 45 miles that day. But many had returned home as they crossed County Wexford, unable

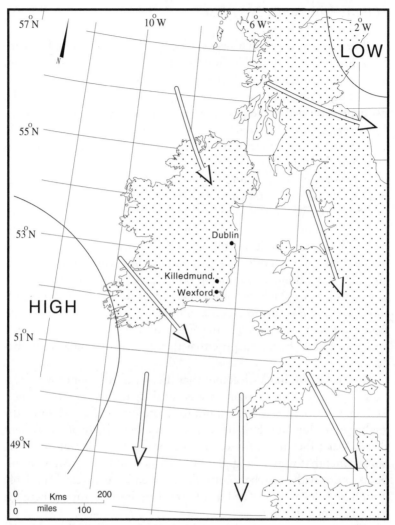

Fig 3.19. Synoptic weather map, 22 June.

to face the privations of the march.

Meanwhile, a larger rebel group that had escaped from Wexford across the river had spent the first night at Peppard's Castle. But many left when it was decided to go northwards into the Wicklow Mountains. About 2,000 remained in the group. Some left to retaliate to yeomanry atrocities near Gorey and perpetuated atrocities of their own. But eventually, led by Anthony Perry, they made a camp at Whiteheaps near Croghan Mountain.

24 JUNE: ACTION AT CASTLECOMER

Castlecomer was a colliery town in County Kilkenny that had a history of insurrection. The Wexfordmen hoped the colliers would join them so they headed towards the Castlecomer plateau.

A ridge of high pressure had been growing in the south since the last depression had moved away (Fig 3.20). The winds on its western flank were light and relatively warm, and being mostly southwesterly had tracked a long distance over the sea. They were so moist that as they cooled during the night mists and fogs developed. Thick foggy weather wrapped itself around the coasts and spread inland, thickening even more as it cooled on climbing over the hills.

When the Wexfordmen broke camp at 2.30am they were shrouded in mist. They may not have known it but they could not have wished for better conditions for attacking Castlecomer. Not only did it hide their approach but the fog persisted a long time into the morning. The anticyclonic conditions produced few breezes to disturb and disperse it. It would linger until the sun broke through the clouds above, causing the mist to evaporate. In fact, at times the visibility was as low as twenty yards. When the Wexfordmen did appear out of the mist they caused such a surprise that they gained the initiative immediately.[76]

It was known in Castlecomer that the Wexford column was nearby, but its large force of yeomen was considered an adequate defence. At 4am, some of these were sent out to reconnoitre. After two miles the fog began to thin and they suddenly saw the main body of rebels right ahead. What they did not see through the fog was the rapid flanking movements that were taking place to their left and right. After an initial skirmish with the rebel centre the yeomen were attacked suddenly from both sides and soon fled, panic-stricken, into the town where the panic became infectious.

The fog continued to clear as this first success was followed up by a full-scale attack on the town. Its resistance lasted for three and a half hours. Then, as a surrender was being negotiated, General Asgill appeared on the hilltops with a force from Kilkenny. They engaged the Wexfordmen long enough to allow the garrison and inhabitants leave, after which the town was abandoned. It was plundered for food and then left burning furiously.

As a military action this had been a great success. The insurgents had captured a reasonably sized, well-defended town; Asgill had been forced to retreat; and the town had provided plenty of food and

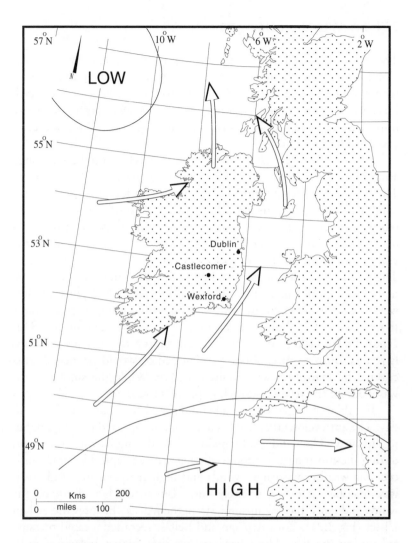

Fig 3.20. Synoptic weather map, 24 June.

supplies. On the other hand, many of the best men had fallen; little in the way of arms and ammunition had been seized; and there were few additional recruits. After so much had gone in their favour, and having seized such a great opportunity, the results were disappointing. For a few hours they pushed on towards County Kildare hoping for more recruits. But few joined them and that night it was decided to return to County Wexford.

25 June: Attack on Hacketstown

The other Wexford rebel army remnants in the east had reached County Wicklow where they rested and were joined by many other rebel groups. With a combined force of 10,000 they decided to attack Hacketstown. Its relative isolation made it an easy target. But more important, it had a supply of weapons and its garrison was a source of continual harassment.

The attack began about 9am. The vast rebel numbers brushed aside the cavalry that was blocking the bridge over the River Dereen. The defenders retreated into their barracks and fortified houses. This combination of positions gave them a wide field of fire to which the rebels were very vulnerable. To counter this, the attackers set the town on fire in several places, creating a thick smoke haze and reducing the visibility. This began to swing the battle in favour of the insurgents. The yeomen and defenders were blinded by the smoke as the fighting raged with greater intensity.[77] Up to 1,500 rebels had guns, so they were well able to match fire with fire. But without a cannon attempts to reduce the stone buildings was limited to setting them on fire. This exposed the attackers to gunfire at a very short range, often with deadly results. Burning carts of hay were pushed by would-be incendiarists covered by mattresses with limited success. While the smoke screen was working the rebels had high hopes of success.

But then the weather took a hand. It had been changing quietly all day. The anticyclone that had been dominant for up to two days began to slip away. The winds had remained light during its withdrawal and during the morning had produced what seemed typical summer anticyclonic weather with light winds and high temperatures. Indeed, it was described as being intensely hot.[78] But in the late afternoon the winds suddenly picked up and strengthened as the pressure fell in Ulster (Fig 3.21). Both Armagh and Belfast recorded a rapid pressure fall during the day. The effect was felt right across Ireland as fresh winds began to blow.

The immediate result was the smoke screen began to disperse in what has been described as 'a high wind'.[79] The yeomen firing from windows began to get a much clearer sight of their targets. The rebels became just as exposed as earlier in the battle and their losses began to mount again. After nine hours fighting their ammunition was low. A victory had been very close, so it was hard, but inevitable, to withdraw. The fighting continued to allow the removal of the dead and wounded. But the garrison's relief was considerable. It was also very short of

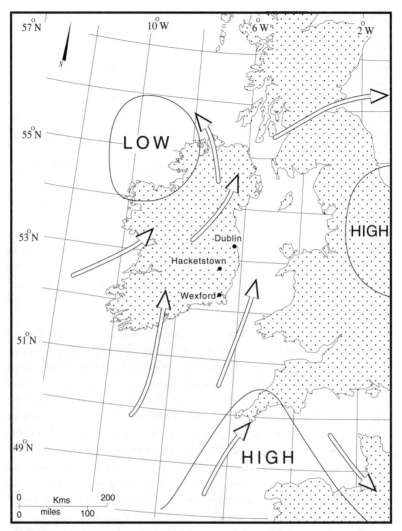

Fig 3.21. Synoptic weather map, 25 June

ammunition and as soon as the rebels left they evacuated the town.

As in Castlecomer, the insurgents had gained a victory of sorts. They had forced the abandonment of Hacketstown, although without knowing it. What they did know was that they had not gained the arms and ammunition they needed. Wind and smoke had won again, ultimately frustrating both sides.

26 June: Surprises in the Fog

The Wexford army in the west marched rapidly back towards the Scullogue Gap. Their journey was at least 30 miles and the day was intensely hot. The heat made this trek even more exhausting than the previous two days.[80] Their fatigue told as they climbed towards the Gap and their progress slowed. Being late in the day, they camped on Kilcomney Hill, still in Carlow. They were so tired that no one noticed the Castlecomer recruits leave. Their one day with the rebels had deflated their enthusiasm. But as they crept away in the darkness they took dozens of the best guns.

During the night mists had formed in the valleys.[81] Having been disturbed briefly by the depression, high pressure returned in the south to produce clear night skies that caused the temperatures to fall sharply (Fig 3.22). The colder, denser air that formed on the high ground rolled into the valleys. There, the condensation and low-lying cloud that resulted produced a dramatic landscape. The waking rebels looked out over a white sea, with islands of high ground protruding here and there.

But they had little time to appreciate the view. They soon discovered the miners and their precious guns had gone. It took longer to discover the threat in the fog. In the early hours, two columns of troops under Asgill that had been following them all the previous day had moved to within a mile. The rebel camp had been spotted some time before when the night air was clear. While the troops waited out of sight, cannon were brought up and an attack prepared. But for the moment they were hidden in the fog. On waking and realising their vulnerability in these weather conditions, the insurgents sent several small patrols out into the fog. They spotted some of the troops and quickly brought back the alarming news. Suddenly the cannon opened up and Asgill mounted his attack.

Being unprepared, and not knowing where the enemy was, flight was the only immediate response possible. The Wexfordmen headed into the Scullogue Gap towards another hill about a mile to the east.[82] Some hoped to defend themselves on higher, more mist-free ground. In other places the mist began to clear as the morning sun burned it away and made the battlefield situation much clearer. However, from the Wexford side more cavalry arrived. To avoid being caught between the two they retreated northwards back into the fog, during which one of their main leaders, Fr John Murphy, became separated from the main body and never regained contact.

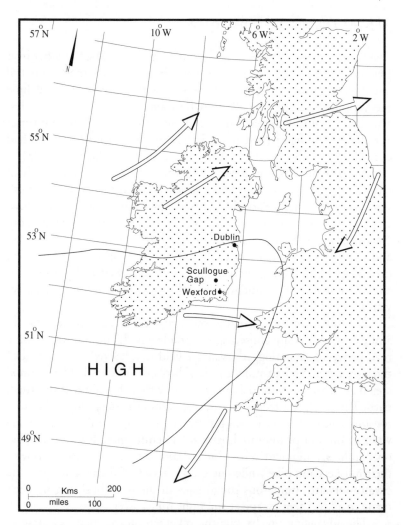

Fig 3.22. Synoptic weather map, 26 June.

It had been a narrow escape. Relief at having escaped was marred by having lost Fr Murphy. The Wexfordmen now split up. One group, keen to end the exhausting forced marches, either returned home or took refuge in the nearby Killoughram Forest. A smaller group, led by Byrne, marched on to Wicklow in a series of night marches to join Perry and Fitzgerald at Whiteheaps, hoping that it would not be long before the French arrived.

30 JUNE: THE BATTLE OF BALLYELLIS

The last few days of June produced much more disturbed weather over Ireland than had occurred for some time. Not only were there more frequent showers of rain, but more persistent frontal rain. On 29 June there had been falls up to half an inch in some parts of Ireland, but less elsewhere.[83] During the early morning the weather was clearing up after a frontal system had passed across Ireland from the southwest, and had cleared most of the country, except the north, by midday (Fig 3.23).

At 10am on Gorey Hill, long after the rain had stopped, Needham received a report of a large body of rebels towards Carnew. As with some of the other relatively isolated towns in County Wicklow, Carnew was an important loyalist outpost with its own garrison. Needham guessed correctly that an attack on the town was intended and sent 200 cavalry to counter the threat. On hearing the rebels were tired and short of ammunition, the patrol followed in hard pursuit, confident of at least intimidating and dispersing them, if not a decisive victory.

Realising they were being pursued the rebels decided on an ambush at a carefully chosen spot at Ballyellis.[84] The site was along a road between a waterlogged, swampy field that backed a dense belt of thornbushes and a half-mile length of broken estate wall. The swampy area had become a formidable barrier now that the rain had returned, particularly as it was fed by the drainage from the steep slopes that rose towards Kilcavan Gap. It was guaranteed to stop the flight of anyone whether on foot or mounted. Around a bend, where it would be seen only at the last moment, a barricade of carts was erected. Most hid with their muskets and pike while one group stayed on the road to draw the cavalry forward, numerous rough gaps in the thornbush having been made to allow them escape at the right time.

The advancing cavalry saw the pikemen on the road in a state of apparent confusion, and charged. Suddenly turning the corner, they faced the barricade and the whole troop piled up as those in front stopped abruptly. The trap was sprung. The rebels opened fire from the sides, while pikemen came round the rear to block any escape. Some who forced their way into the field were caught in the heaviness of the bog and were easily taken and killed. The rain had ensured there was no escape that way.

This was a significant victory for the insurgents. It resulted in a most welcome supply of arms, ammunition and equipment, especially as a later attack on Carnew failed to realise any. The victory was dou-

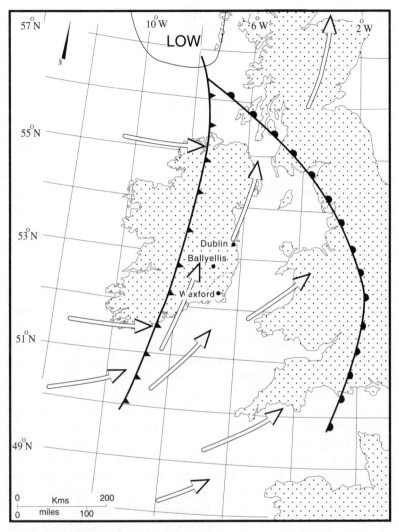

Fig 3.23. Synoptic weather map, 30 June.

bly welcome as it was against one of the most hated regiments. It gave
an incalculable boost to the morale of the insurgents at a time when
they were on the defensive.

The westerly wind carried the sound of the gunfire to Gorey
where, on Gorey Hill, Needham became worried and decided to lead
another patrol out. Meeting two survivors and learning the shocking
news, he decided to focus his forces on the defence of Gorey in case it
should also be attacked.

4

JULY: THE WEATHER IN DECLINE

All the evidence points to the month of July being remarkably wet. Rainfall totals for the month as a whole at Belfast (117.6mm), Dublin (84.1mm) and Edgeworthstown (161.8mm) show that July had exceptional rainfall.[1] For Dublin and Edgeworthstown, July was the wettest month, not just of the summer, but for the entire year (Fig 4.1). Nearly every other day had some rain and in Belfast two-thirds of the days were wet.

Throughout the month the pressure pattern was quite different from that of June (Fig 4.2). A string of depressions tracked eastwards introducing belts of rain, often on successive days. As a result there were longer continuous periods of westerlies than in the previous month extending southwards as far as the west coast of France. These confined the French fleets at Brest and Rochelle to port and frustrated the Irish exiles who were there hoping to be part of an invasion of Ireland.

During the month the Wicklow Mountains became the focus of the United Irish campaign. On Dublin's doorstep, these mountains loomed over the city as a constant but ill-defined threat. In Dublin Castle there was a keen awareness of this, but in the rebel camps there was no plan to attack the capital directly. Indeed, there was no clear rebel strategy at all. During the month it was to vacillate between guerrilla tactics, building up military capability, campaigning in the midlands and conserving resources while awaiting the French.

There were only two environments that provided some measure of protection for the rebels while waiting for the French: the bog lands of the midlands, where the rebels led by William Aylmer were contained, and the mountainous parts of Wicklow, where encirclement was very difficult, cavalry of little use and lack of roads hindered deployment, especially of artillery.[2] Away from the roads, they were little known. A summary view concludes, '… the tract of country now occupied by the rebels … has long been and continues to be as little known to us as any of the wildest parts of America; a rude and barren expanse of heath, moor, bog and mountain, it has been hitherto considered as scarcely

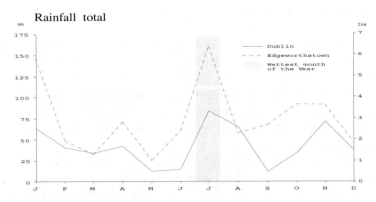

Fig 4.1. *Dublin and Edgeworthstown monthly rainfall totals, 1798*

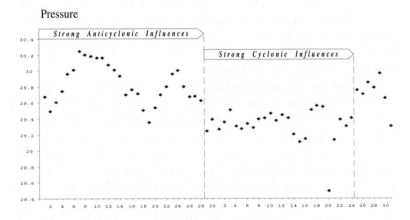

Fig 4.2. *Daily pressure at Armagh, June and July 1798.*

penetrable by the most adventurous sportsman'.[3] Interestingly, the description omits the wooded parts that were often on the lower, less remote slopes.

Where both the terrain and the weather favoured mobility and pursuit the insurgents were always at a severe disadvantage. However, in the mountains exposure and rain hindered government forces and helped the insurgents become invisible. The Wicklow leader, Joseph Holt, was based at Whelp Rock, near Blessington. This was one of several Wicklow camps that received refugees from other counties, especially Wexford. In addition, it became a springboard for offensives into the midlands.

5 July: Blinded by Fog

A warm front had passed over Ireland late in the day of 4 July. This brought yet more rain to add to a succession of wet days. But it also brought warm air from the tropics and temperatures began to rise again, even though the pressure was persistently low (Fig 4.3). The warm front also brought mist and fog. From the Wexford coast to the British fleet off Brittany, an extensive haze covered the sea, at times becoming very thick.[4]

On the southern edge of the Wicklow Hills, Whiteheaps had become an important rebel camp. Here, as the front approached and cloud built up during the evening, the light failed early and the night promised to be long and uncomfortable. But it brought a happier moment to dispel the gloom as the remnants of the two columns that had escaped Lake at Wexford were reunited.[5] Time for celebration and conviviality was limited. A lengthy stay in one place increased the chances of discovery. So far they had eluded the net Needham was drawing round them. The rebels were aware of his tactics and were set to head further into the mountains.

Even while they celebrated their reunion, Needham was deploying a strong force to attack their camp at dawn. As he surrounded their camp he also occupied high ground in case he had to pursue them. From there the rebels would be conspicuous as they moved in the narrow valley confines, even if they were wooded. On finding many of the hillslopes were only covered with heather Needham thought his task would be even easier than he had anticipated. So he had high hopes of a decisive victory.

Before dawn, after the rain had stopped, the rebels left camp. The rain had wet the ground thoroughly. It was replaced by a dense fog as the ground warmed in the early morning sun. With visibility down to 20 feet, the rebels moved slowly, trying to stay together while remaining alert for Needham's troops.[6] The fog was now exerting a powerful influence on events.[7] Needham attacked the campsite at dawn but found it empty. He had not missed the rebels by much, but he could not see where they were. Word came that they were moving towards the Wicklow Gap. Needham found the fog made it impossible to use the advantage of the high ground and his directions became guesswork. At one stage the rebels heard musket-fire from Needham's men ahead of them. Thus warned, but without sight of them, they turned southwards away from the danger.

The sun climbed higher in the sky and the fog evaporated. As it

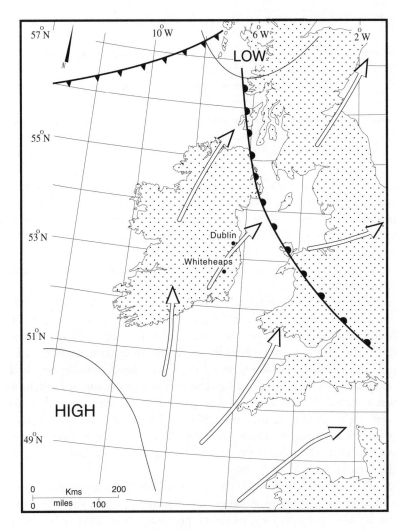

Fig 4.3. Synoptic weather map, 5 July.

did so, the rebels saw General Duff's cavalry. Instead of taking flight they surprised Duff by attacking ferociously, forcing him back towards Ballygullen. But large reinforcements arrived from Needham and to avoid encirclement the rebels made a tactical withdrawal, during which they became fragmented.[8] Some headed northwards to the mountains, while a large number retreated to Carrigrew Hill (from where many eventually accepted the amnesty terms that Cornwallis later announced).

9 JULY: THE EXPEDITION INTO THE MIDLANDS

Several thousand Wexfordmen joined Holt's camp at Whelp Rock near Blessington. In a major debate on strategy Holt proposed a guerilla campaign in Wicklow. The alternative was to join Alymer's army at Timahoe in County Kildare and then march on to join the Ulster rebels, as proposed by Fr Kearns. Kearns narrowly won the vote, although Michael Dwyer and other Wicklowmen remained and went to Glenmalure.[9]

The reasons behind this decision are not clear. Holt felt Kearn's plan underestimated the environment into which they would be taking their struggle. He saw the move as leaving 'a strong country where we could have made a good resistance and obtained terms, and moved into an open one'.[10] Byrne expressed his doubt about the wisdom of such a move when he reflected 'I could never learn the real motive which induced these leaders to quit the Wicklow Mountains and march with the Wexford division ... into open country like Kildare, Meath, Louth etc'.[11]

The countryside where they were heading provided little shelter and cover compared with what they were leaving. Away from the mountains they would need to move quickly to maintain any element of surprise. But out in the bogs the roads cut up easily when wet, making long journeys exhausting and slow. There, rapid mobility required reasonably dry weather as well as reasonably remote routes. Perhaps it was assumed the weather would be good, even though it had deteriorated a great deal since the fine weather of May and June. It is not surprising that several historians have concluded that the Kildare option was not properly thought through and was probably carried because of the forceful manner of Kearns.[12]

A trough of low pressure had produced some cloudy overcast skies and intermittently rainy weather. On 8 June the rain paused and the day became quite pleasant while the preparations to leave went ahead in a flurry of activity. Most of the insurgents had to carry their own equipment and supplies. As they rested that night the clouds thickened once again. There was to be little respite from the rain. Another frontal system crossed into Ireland the following day in the form of a broad band of rain that extended from Scotland to Brittany (Fig 4.4). It passed over Wicklow during the morning when the insurgents set out. By this time the Wexfordmen may have been longing to leave the mountains because since their arrival there they had experienced much wetter weather than they were used to in Wexford. But after it had passed and everyone was thoroughly wet, pleasant warm air flooded

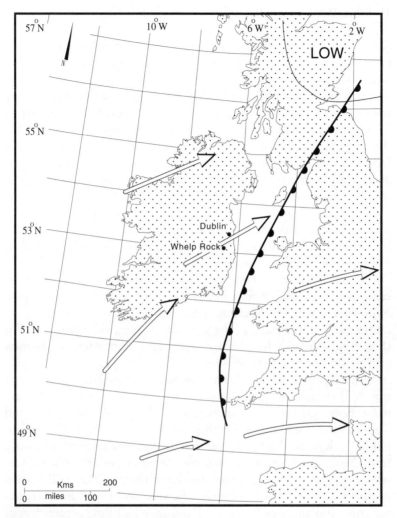

Fig 4.4. Synoptic weather map, 9 July.

into Ireland, just for a while.

Having left the hills they avoided the shortest route for one less used by the military, although the weather made an encounter even less likely. They reached central Kildare by nightfall.[13] But many were soon having second thoughts. The persistently poor weather and the tough going caused fatigue and many desertions before reaching the camp at Timahoe.[14]

10 July: Arrival at Timahoe

Kearns led his army from their temporary camp across the Curragh towards Timahoe. This landscape is particularly open and exposed, but in crossing the permeable limestones of the Curragh it was drier underfoot and easier to march across than the bogs ahead of them. Using trackways to Robertstown and Prosperous they finally arrived at Timahoe late in the evening. The details of the route are uncertain but the distance involved was about 35 miles. This was yet another long fatiguing trek that called for huge resources of stamina and perseverance. They were not spotted by any military – a particular danger as they skirted around the garrison town of Newbridge, bisected the routes from Dublin to the south and crossed the Grand Canal. The weather also held up. It was dry most of the day with a warm wind from the south behind them (Fig 4.5). If fortune favours the bold, then it was smiling on them intensely.

The 1,500 men at Timahoe were not expecting them. Once the camp had been one of four in Kildare, with several thousand men. Now there was only one camp. Their active campaign had ended on 20 June after a heavy defeat, the same day as Wexford capitulated. For three weeks Alymer had been negotiating a surrender, so the new arrivals did not fit into their plans.[15]

The Wexford-Wicklow army was not an impressive sight. Having stumbled through the bogs on the last leg of their journey they were worn, bedraggled and looked wretched.[16] They had few supplies and were short of ammunition for their desperate adventure. Kearns had hoped to draw the Kildaremen into his plans, but sought little advice from them.[17] Such an attitude was not likely to recruit the Kildaremen, who were also short of supplies and ammunition. They still harried nearby routes between Dublin and the west and raided mail coaches for arms. But this was for survival and they had little expectation of changing the balance of power in Kildare.

Together the two groups totalled about 4,000, the largest number that had been in the camp during the campaign. This was both a potential strength and a weakness. The bogs of Kildare did not provide much food. Since this had already been a problem for the smaller camp, it would be even more significant for a much larger one. The camp's strength had always been its remoteness and defensibility, rather than its convenience for supplies. Timahoe was also a village on a gravel island in a vast sodden desert called the Bog of Allen, from which emerged the rivers Boyne (to the north) and Barrow (to the

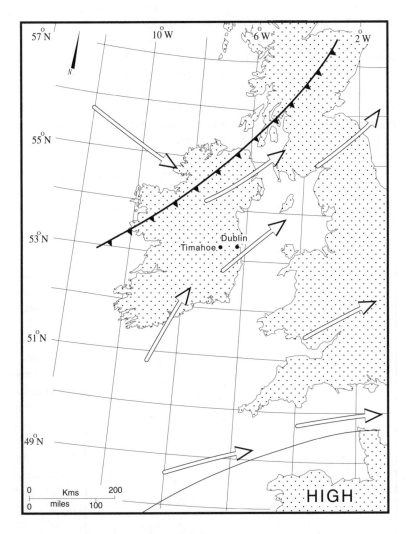

Fig 4.5. Synoptic weather map, 10 July.

south). The village could produce a limited amount of food, but most was acquired by raiding the small number of villages further afield.

As Kearns' army rested that night they would have been aware that there was little to gain by staying at Timahoe. Late in the afternoon the rain returned. Yet more rain was to follow and as it fell the men huddled under what cover they could find and waited for a drier, more hopeful dawn.

11 JULY: ENGAGEMENT AT CLONARD BRIDGE

About 9am the insurgents left Timahoe. The unusually late hour to begin a day's march may have been due to the weather. A family of depressions was passing over Ireland and before dawn yet another warm front had brought its miserable, misty rain across the boglands (Fig 4.6). But it gave way to fresher air free of the haze and cloud of the previous day. Not that there was much to see since the flat terrain provided few vantage points.

The target was Clonard, to capture arms and ammunition. Their route took them to a toll bridge across the River Boyne. Close to the bridge was a stone house occupied by Richard Tyrrell with about 40 yeomanry.[18] Warned of the rebels' approach, they took up defensive positions in the house and a tower built into the courtyard wall.

Initially, the rebel cavalry approaching the house from the east was fired on with considerable success and forced to retreat (Fig 4.7). Tyrrell had placed his best marksmen in the tower and the upper house in order to

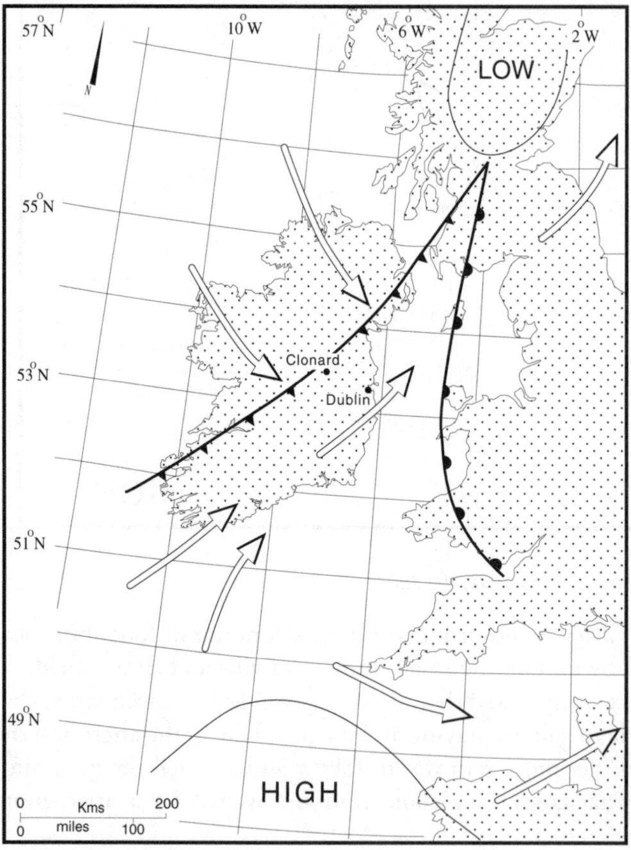

Fig 4.6. Synoptic weather map, 11 July.

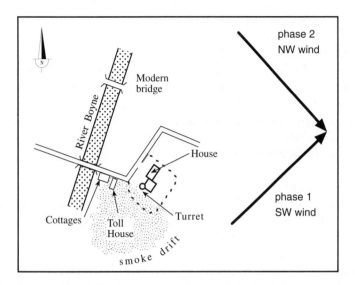

Fig 4.7. Wind and smoke at the battle of Clonard.

overlook the bridge. Since the house commanded the bridge the insurgents had no choice but to capture it before crossing. Although the tower was set on fire, four of the six musketeers inside managed to escape to the house, covered by dense smoke drifting towards it.[19] The nearby cottages were also set on fire, their damp thatch producing thick smoke that added significantly to what was already swirling about. If all this smoke had screened the bridge from the house it would have covered the insurgents as they crossed. But its failure to serve the rebels as well as it had the retreating musketeers lies in its direction as well as its thickness. The attack commenced when the wind was from the southwest. Hence the dense smoke drifted from the tower towards the house in the early part of the action. But when the cold front passed over about noon the wind veered to the northwest and blew away from the bridge and the house, leaving them relatively clear (Fig 4.7). If the cottages were set on fire early in the action there could only have been a short period when the smoke would have provided cover to cross the bridge. But at that stage their attention was focused on the yeomen.[20]

After six hours of fighting, about 5pm, relief arrived for Tyrrell and his men.[21] It is possible that the rebels were already carrying out an orderly retreat since their ammunition was getting low. This was a serious setback for the rebels. They had failed in their objectives and had suffered heavy losses.

12 July: Dispersed at Rynville Hill

As the insurgents camped for the night a new depression was arriving (Fig 4.8). The last one had quickly reached the North Sea to give way to its successor. The pressure in the north fell even further. In practical terms this merely added to the misery of the summer. The warm front brought misty rain during the early morning, even thick fog along the Dublin coast.[22] The rain was widespread, extending from Wexford to Donegal. There was little shelter from the weather for the rebel army and they were constantly wet.[23] As the latest front moved away the winds changed direction to bring warm sector air from the south and southwest. This time the change in wind was to assist the rebels during the day.

Lieutenant-Colonel Gough was now pursuing them and found 'their march was easily traced as they left the country in flames as they passed'.[24] He caught up with them at Rynville Hill where they had halted to prepare food. After the battle many boiling pots with supplies of flour, groceries, wine and spirits, as well as half-skinned bullocks and sheep, were found.

The insurgents had a strong position on top of a wide low hill. On seeing Gough's force they quickly formed a line across the cornfields around the hill. Outnumbered, Gough considered his position to be weak.[25] But the rebels stood their ground defiantly and aggressively, certain that their vastly superior numbers would carry the day. Gough's men attacked and fired rapidly and accurately into the insurgents' lines. These were so packed that they were easy targets. The rebels' certainty and aggression appeared to vanish. They could have made their numbers tell by charging with their pikes. Their weariness has been suggested as one reason for why they did not, but that is unlikely to have caused such a rapid change once the battle had started.[26] Instead they hurried away in some confusion. They may have realised the inadequacies of their position. The hilltop did not offset the openness of the terrain and the firmness of the ground. The bogs had been left behind and the battle was being fought on good agricultural ground on which Gough's cavalry, although hampered by ditches and banks, were more effective than in the bogs and mountains.[27]

Holt thought that Gough's forces, particularly the cavalry, might be countered by smoke.[28] Perhaps the experience of the previous day gave him the idea. So he had the roadside houses set on fire. Since the weather had been so wet they burned with a dense smoke that drifted thickly across the battlefield and provided a screen for their withdrawal. They

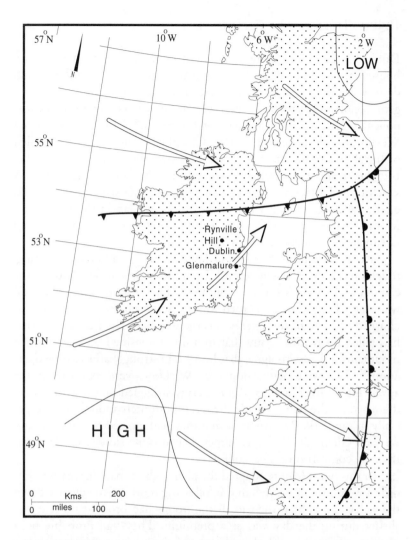

Fig 4.8. Synoptic weather map, 12 July.

retreated northwards, the smoke following them from the south. As a result many escaped. The weather improved so much that, away from the smoke, Holt was able to use the sun to find his direction.[29] But the rebels had taken a serious blow and had lost much of their supplies. Fatigue from constant marching and fighting in poor weather took its toll as an increasing number of stragglers fell behind and were cut down by the following cavalry.

12 July: The Sweep of Glenmalure

Dublin Castle feared a drawn-out guerilla war. A scenario of attacks on houses, farms and mail coaches as well as muggings and murder, would destroy the rural economy and lead to political instability and insurgent opportunism if the French were to arrive. Therefore, it became policy to take the offensive against the rebels.[30] Moore moved from Wexford to join Lake and Colonel Campbell in an attack on the Glen of Imaal, where the main body of Wicklow rebels was thought to be. But they heard the rebels had moved into the Glenmalure valley. A synchronised attack was agreed whereby Lake blocked the eastern end of the valley, Campbell went to the Wicklow Gap in the north, and Moore hauled himself over Table Mountain, to drive along Glenmalure from above (Fig 4.9).

Moore set out on the night of 11 June. His men found 'marching' tough on the steep, boggy terrain. Even more difficult was hauling the cannon and supplies up the mountain. 'The ground except the road was everywhere a bog', recorded Moore, and even that track was soon churned up.[31] A greater enemy was the weather. The frontal rain that had fallen on Kearns' army that morning intensified on reaching the mountains. Historians agree that heavy rain strongly affected the operation.[32] The west-facing slopes of Wicklow were exposed to the advancing weather, and as Moore's army struggled upwards they were drenched by the rain. It made the terrain infinitely more hostile, especially in the dark. By early morning they had crossed the summit and were on Glenmalure's upper slopes. Dawn came slowly. Its light was the only comfort on a wet, cold day.

At this point Moore adapted the plan to the appalling weather. His orders were to wait until 4am the following morning to advance down the valley. To lighten their loads the troops had brought no tents, so shelter during the day was at a premium. They had probably been unaware of just how bleak and exposed these mountains were. After using what natural cover was available and having had some food and rest, the men were relatively refreshed. So Moore decided to begin the sweep at 6pm instead of waiting until the morning.[33] Besides the wetness and the cold, Moore reasoned that such a narrow valley could be held by a small force if they had time to assemble. It must be remembered that many of the Wicklow rebels were no longer in the mountains but had joined the campaign into County Kildare. Most notably Holt, who became Moore's chief protagonist later in July, had reluctantly left the mountains on that campaign, but survived and returned

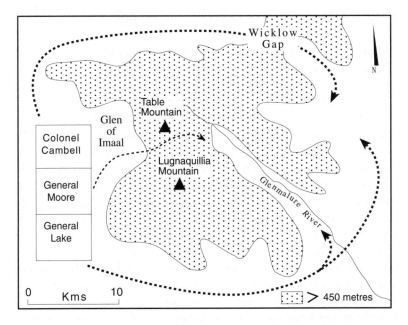

Fig 4.9. The attack on Glenmalure.

very quickly to the environment he knew so well. His appointment as the leader in Wicklow is considered to have been largely a result of his familiarity with the terrain (in all weathers) rather than his specifically military skills. For five hours he combed the valley. The rain made the visibility poor and when it eased off mists swirled round the summits and higher slopes. But in the end they found nothing. The weather certainly helped any rebels escaping across the mountains, but it is unlikely many were there at all. Their apparent elusiveness was frustrating.

The troops had suffered in the mountains. The failure to carry tents had been a mistake. Without shelter from the heavy rain and the coldness that penetrated their bones, their health suffered. Even Moore succumbed to a fever.[34] It confirmed, if confirmation was necessary, that the Wicklow Mountains were an inhospitable wilderness, even in the summer.

14 July: A Bombardment at Knightstown Bog

Although the depression and associated fronts that had been active on 12 July had moved away, it rained again on 14 July when the insurgents drive to the north was halted at Knightstown Bog. The day was wet throughout Ireland as another warm front introduced moist air from the south (Fig 4.10). This air had been modified a great deal as it travelled northwards, having followed a wide curving track that brought it to Ireland from almost a westerly direction. It had cooled all the way from its source west of the Bay of Biscay and Portugal. The front was heralded by very cloudy weather, so it did little to raise the temperatures and the sun was not very effective in penetrating the masses of cloud that layered the sky. The mildness of this weather was altogether better for the daily forced marches the Wexford army now endured, compared with the intense heat of the early summer. However, to the undernourished and rest-deprived insurgents the rain was no longer refreshing but added to their exhaustion and fatigue.

General Meyrick from Navan and General Weyms from Drogheda had taken up the pursuit. After a brief overnight stop in the rain near Slane the rebels continued northwards soon after dawn. They were harried from behind and from time to time groups of insurgents unable to keep up were caught and cut down, while others tried to break away and escape on their own. The pursuit came to a climax about 11am, north of Navan. About 1,500 rebels were on a rise between two areas of Knightstown Bog. They formed a line, charged the pursuing cavalry and succeeded in forcing them back.[35] But they had neither the arms nor the strength to achieve a victory before the main body arrived in support.

Since the bog was relatively small the reinforcements were deployed around most of the bog's perimeter. The rebels found a good defensive position in a defile between the two areas of bog.[36] To counter this and to avoid high casualties from attacking such a position, Weyms brought his artillery forward and bombarded it. The insurgents had little shelter from such an onslaught and were driven into the bog. Their only hope was to break through the cordon. The bog was by no means a completely open landscape. Its thickets and brushwood provided some temporary concealment as they tried to break out. Although large numbers were killed, many escaped, especially towards the southeast and northeast.[37]

But they were a broken force. Of those who survived the battle and its aftermath, large numbers were arrested, court-martialled and

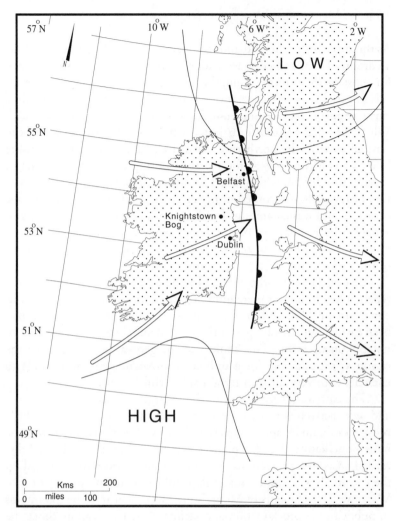

Fig 4.10. Synoptic weather map, 14 July.

executed. Others negotiated terms that the more conciliatory policy of Cornwallis now permitted. Some tried to head back towards Wicklow, regretting the decision ever to leave its protection, while others took refuge in the cornfields, ditches and other hiding places. The search for them went on for many days as troops scoured the countryside to find them. Fatigue and exhaustion had finally taken their toll.

16 JULY: MOUNTAIN REFUGES IN WICKLOW

As the survivors of the midlands campaign struggled back to Wicklow, a curtain of rain and cold descended on the mountains and remained for most of the month. A number of the depressions responsible for this lingered for some time as they crossed the country. Even within a small country like Ireland quite large contrasts in weather resulted. When the spell began on 16 July a depression appears to have been centred close to the northern coast of Ireland and the actual pressure levels were at their lowest for any time during the month (Fig 4.11). During this period, which lasted about ten days, some of the rain was very heavy. Belfast recorded nearly an inch of rain in 24 hours on one occasion, an unusual amount for the month of July. The weather also brought the midday temperatures below 16^0C, which is low for the month of July. In addition, several diary entries noted the coldness of the period.[38]

During late July the mountains became the last refuge for the rebels. They could rest there unmolested, raiding for their food. In this environment, Holt and his men felt secure. One major operation had been carried out already against them in Glenmalure and that had been notably unsuccessful. This confirmed the general impression that the region was unsuitable for a military campaign, being impossible to encircle, with very difficult terrain and awful weather.

The case for a speedy end to the insurgency was as strong as ever and was actively pursued by Cornwallis. He saw there was little prospect of a quick and complete military solution and, desiring to be more conciliatory than his predecessor, he had proclaimed in all disturbed areas that protections would be given to those who handed up their arms. It was hoped that this would lead to the pacification of Wicklow. Detachments of Moore's men were sent into the mountains to publicise the proclamation and facilitate the pacification. Since the vast tracts of bogs on the mountains limited the locations where the insurgents could live, a strategy was developed whereby a number of detachments would camp in the glens and other habitable parts to make contact and offer the amnesty. However, where this was refused the strength of the military machine would be used.

The new policy could not be used in the mountains immediately because of the appalling weather. But that was less of a problem elsewhere. Although it was uncomfortably cold, the rain in these other areas was more broken. Thus contact with the rebels was sought in the accessible areas.[39] But Moore found the main obstacle to the new

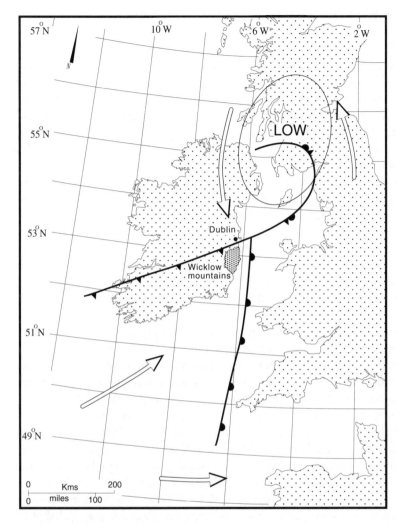

Fig 4.11. Synoptic weather map, 16 July.

policy was the local yeomen who were set on revenge regardless of the proclamation. So his deployments were as much to prevent their excesses as against the rebels.

The enforced delay to operations in the mountains had a number of welcome benefits. The troops had been seriously fatigued by the weather and needed time to recover.[40] There was also time to refit. When the weather did clear there was a refreshed, better-equipped force to finish the job.

26 July: The Second Glenmalure Offensive

The rain could not go on forever. Moore knew the time would come when he would be able to take his campaign back into the mountains under vastly improved conditions.[41] What he had been waiting for arrived on 26 July. The rain stopped, at last. Yet another depression had crossed Ireland, this time taking a more southerly track towards England. But this was followed by westerly air from a ridge of high pressure pushing northwards towards Ireland (Fig 4.12). Although it was still cloudy, the air was much more stable and the temperatures were noticeably warmer. The successive waves of rain that had crossed the country day after day for some time past came to an end. Now was the moment to take the offensive again.

Moore brought one regiment into Glenmalure from the direction of Seven Churches and another two up the valley from the direction of Rathdrum. Holt had about 500 men in the valley, but they had the initiative as they knew the valley so well. When they learned of Moore's move they took up advantageous positions to fire on the advancing troops. This soon stopped Moore's advance. The narrow valley limited his troop's mobility, the cavalry could not be deployed and it was difficult to manoeuvre the artillery. But the insurgents also had problems. They knew the terrain and were more mobile, but they had little in the way of arms and ammunition for a pitched battle. Inevitably, therefore, Holt decided on a strategic retreat up the mountainside. As they retreated they could see Moore's troops swarming below and could have caused heavy casualties had they had the necessary firepower. This would have dissuaded any further adventures into the wilderness by their pursuers. Instead they descended to the western side of Table Mountain into the Glen of Imaal, 1,500 ft below.[42]

Moore's account of this and subsequent actions is a picture of almost constant pursuit. Over the next few days this was probably the case. While the weather allowed he had detachments of troops in the valleys and patrols on the mountains, driving the rebels from place to place, giving little respite and denying them necessary subsistence.[43] The rain was not long in returning, but by this time Moore's troops were well placed and it was much more difficult for the insurgents to keep out of their way. Increasing numbers gave up, especially when they eventually heard of the amnesty.

Nevertheless, Holt kept a large number together. The realisation that the army was no longer prepared to leave them unmolested in their mountain sanctuaries undoubtedly came as a blow. To combat

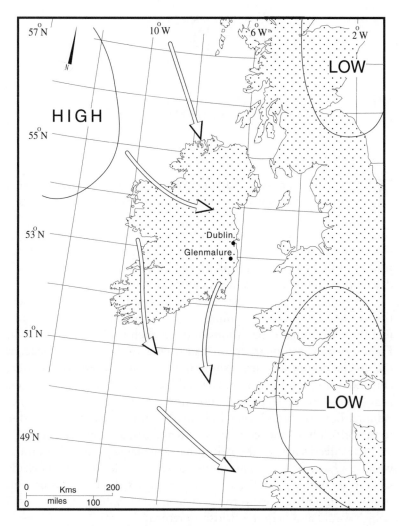

Fig 4.12. Synoptic weather map, 26 July.

this he decided that they needed to become much more mobile than in the past when they had always seemed several days ahead of their pursuers. When the weather had been poor it had been easy to stay ahead, but it was difficult when the weather was good. A long summer was ahead of them and the weather could only be expected to improve. But they still hoped to hold out until the French arrived.

5

AUGUST: A SECOND SUMMER

The first three weeks of August had very mixed weather. Despite a series of depressions ensuring that rain occurred at regular intervals the weather became warmer and pressure was higher than in July (Figs 5.1 and 5.2). At the end of August a 'second summer' arrived, especially in the west, that was similar to the golden period of May-June. During that time atmospheric pressure rose further and the midday temperatures were a comfortable 18-20^{0}C.

An important part of the 1798 story took place in France where the weather also played a significant role. Throughout the early summer there were high expectations of the French landing in Ireland. In France, two expeditionary forces had been assembled. In Rochelle, at the Rochefort docks, three ships under Commodore Savary were embarking 1,000 troops under General Humbert. Meanwhile, in Brest a larger fleet of nine ships and 3,000 troops had been assembled under Admiral Bompard and General Hardy. But there were still delays due to the British blockade, contrary winds and disputes over payment.[1]

The effectiveness of the British blockade largely depended on the weather.[2] Easterly winds and moderate weather allowed the blockade to keep its position off Brest. In westerly gales the fleet sheltered in nearby Falmouth knowing the French needed easterly winds to sail (which would also help the British to return).

It was intended that the two fleets should leave at the same time.[3] A third fleet under General Kilmaine had originally been intended. This was to have been much larger than the others, but it never materialised.[4] It was a tragedy for the rebels' cause that General Humbert landed in County Mayo in time to benefit from a 'second summer' but with the much larger military force still stranded by the weather in Brest, waiting for suitable winds. The successes achieved after landing, with relatively small losses to the French, needed following up if the British hold on Ireland was to be weakened. So the month ended with a mixture of triumph and anxiety, and much sunshine.

Pressure

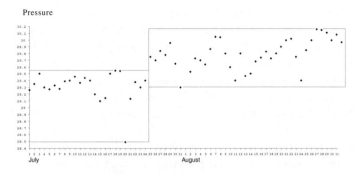

Fig 5.1 Atmospheric pressure for Armagh Observatory July-August 1798

Raindays

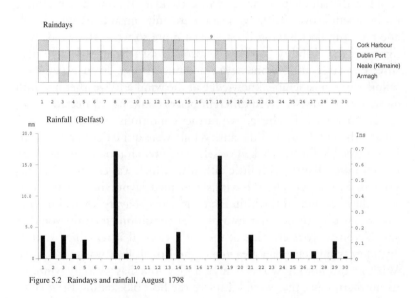

Figure 5.2   Raindays and rainfall, August 1798

Fig 5.2 Raindays and rainfall, August 1798

93

6 August: Departure from Rochelle

Commodore Savary managed to escape to sea unobserved by any of the British fleet prowling off the French coast. He had three ships, over 1,000 troops and four light field pieces. His departure from Rochelle was made possible by a change from westerly to easterly winds in the Bay of Biscay. Savary must have contemplated his departure with satisfaction as these winds took him far westwards into the Atlantic.

While the weather was favourable at Rochelle, it was quite different in Brest. The departures from both ports were intended to be simultaneous, to ensure both parts of the expedition arrived about the same time. Such co-ordinated planning required particularly suitable weather. Sometimes an easterly wind occurred over most of the western coast of France, from Brittany to Bordeaux. But early August 1798 was not one of these. The anticyclone over the Bay of Biscay produced contrasting weather along the coastline (Fig 5.3). The winds were offshore in the south, but the clockwise circulation around it produced onshore winds over Brittany. These were quite unsuitable for a blockade-breaking fleet leaving Brest – even more so when the winds were light and the visibility good, as is normally associated with high pressure. But large anticyclones were not understood. Even experienced sailors with considerable knowledge of the wind and weather had little awareness of how winds in different places could be connected.

As Savary left Rochelle, two further conditions were in his favour. Firstly, the winds around the anticyclone were quite light and relatively comfortable for the packed vessels. The French took their vessels far out into the Atlantic with little difficulty, which was exactly what they wanted. From Rochelle the winds remained favourable for five days until they became calm within the anticyclone. Savary knew, however, that when they turned northwards (and conditions for this would be suitable on the western side of the anticyclone if it remained stationary) they would enter an area where the British fleet was more active. What he did not know was that an anticyclone has westerly winds on its northern flank that would displace the fleet blockading Brest closer to the coast. In so far as this cleared the way for Savary, it did just the opposite for the second expedition in Brest.

The fleet in Brest was ready to sail. But it was demanding payment by the Directory in Paris of money promised to the crew and troops, as well as money for additional stores. This dispute had remained unresolved for some time and there was little prospect of setting sail until it was. Humbert had similar delays in Rochelle, but had settled the

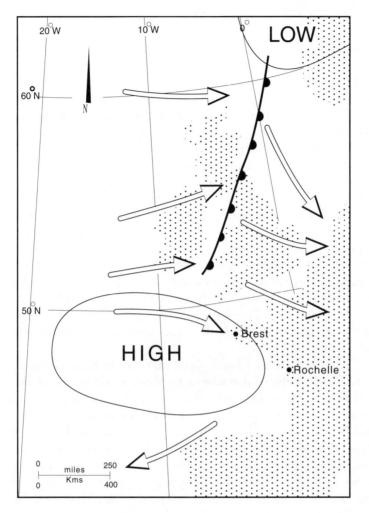

Fig 5.3. Synoptic weather map, 6 August.

matter personally and hurried his expedition to sea.[5] So they were on their own. As the expedition turned northwards, the pressure pattern changed, the high pressure moved away and the winds became more northerly. Progress was slow and uncomfortable (especially for the troops). But the measure of their strategy's success was that they managed to avoid any British frigates.

21 AUGUST: SEA BREEZES IN DONEGAL BAY

The French arrived in Donegal Bay from the west at a time when Ireland was enjoying a spell of very fine weather. Atmospheric pressure had been rising for some days and any of those on board would not have thought it greatly dissimilar from western France (Fig 5.4).

Their instructions were to land on the south Donegal, Sligo or north Mayo coast, according to the wind direction. There is a tradition that months before Lord Edward Fitzgerald, the leader of the United Irishmen, with others that included a French navy captain, had visited Killala to consider its suitability.[6] Retrospectively, some of the French thought that Killala was an ill-chosen place, being in the wildest part of Ireland with little apparent preparation for a rising, among peasants who had never heard of the French.[7] A local view was that landing at a more suitable place could have produced a different outcome. But it was a fateful decision to land in Killala. Within seven weeks two other expeditions arrived in search of Humbert's landing place. Both headed to Donegal, one missing the chance to rescue the French remnant in Killala. A landing in Donegal would have placed Humbert's campaign in the north of Ireland. Whether that would have been more successful is conjectural.

The wind played a highly significant part in the decision to land in Killala. It is known that adverse northerly winds frustrated the original plan to go to Donegal.[8] But the winds over Ireland had been southerly for some days, due to the high pressure over eastern Ireland and Britain. The northerly winds responsible for the diversion could have been due to a depression far to the northwest, a few days' sail away from Donegal. This may have frustrated an attempt to reach a relatively high latitude before turning and approaching Donegal from the northwest, thereby avoiding being seen from land until the last possible moment. There is evidence for this since in the northwestern seas off Ireland, the frigate *Cerberus* logged strong northerly winds on the 12-17 and 20 August.[9] Undoubtedly, Savary would have encountered these as well, so they may be part of the story.

But there is another, more likely, explanation. In Donegal Bay the ships encountered a land-sea breeze system. These occur in fine weather with light winds. They are landward during the day and become seaward in the evening as the land cools relative to the warm sea surface. Matthew Tone's account fits this explanation exactly. Initially, the ships sailed across the bay towards their preferred landing place: 'We stood up towards Killybegs harbour with a light breeze and got within

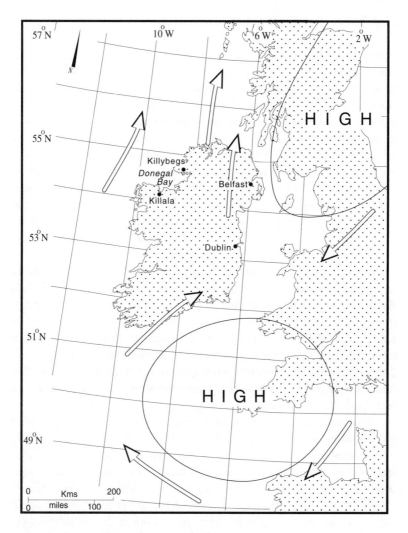

Fig 5.4. Synoptic weather map, 21 August.

two hours' sail of our landing place when the wind died away. This is dammed unlucky and has entirely deprived us of the advantage of surprise. The wind springing up contrary in the evening, we stood right across the bay to the County Mayo, where Killala, I believe, affords a place proper to debark. Night, and the want of a pilot obliges us to anchor in the middle of the bay.'[10]

22 August: The French Land at Killala

It was clear and starlit as the French waited for dawn. To land during the night without local help was to court disaster. Armagh observatory noted that the night had been as beautiful as the day. The dawn heralded another idyllic summer's day. It was calm and hot, with brilliant sunshine.[11] Matthew Tone wrote: 'This morning we are under way again, endeavouring to get into Killala, the wind not very good – we are in sight of both Killybegs and Killala without the power of entering either ... We are surrounded on all sides by very high hills; if there is an aristocrat within ten leagues of us, he is with his glass – watching our motions and sending expresses in every direction – these are pleasant speculations. I hope the rogues won't have the wit to destroy all the fishing boats round the bay, for we are in great need of some to help us to debark.'[12]

They still had a struggle in the morning when the light southerly wind of the anticyclonic circulation slowed their progress into Killala Bay (Fig 5.5). There was no prospect of reaching Donegal without further delays and the certainty of being intercepted. So they landed at Kilcummin Head, five miles north of Killala, at 3pm, with the aid of some fishermen.[13] Tone was right to think they were being watched. Being larger than most ships entering the bay they drew attention. The ruse of flying the English flag reassured some, but the yeomanry remained under arms the whole day.

The landing point had near-horizontal rock strata that provided good landing and docking conditions for the rowing boats, especially in a calm sea. It was also obscured from Killala by low hills. Immediately General Sarrazin and a local man who had sailed with them, Henry O'Kane, led the cavalry to Killala. Another officer, Captain Jobit, displayed an awareness of the severe weather that could afflict this coast, noting that 'The men, women and children were almost naked and have no other shelter than a small wretched cabin, which gives no protection against the severity of the weather'.[14] However, as yet he had not encountered it himself.

In fact, it was on 'a fine summer's evening' that about 50 yeomen and fencibles of the Prince of Wales Regiment were drawn up to oppose them on a low ridge outside Killala.[15] After a skirmish they retired into the town and were pursued into the 'castle' before surrendering. Killala's small harbour became a hive of activity as stores, ammunition and military equipment were brought across the bay from Kilcummin in fishermen's boats, supplementing the pony traffic and

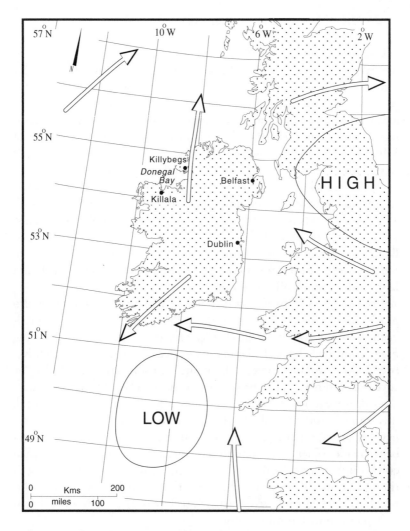

Fig 5.5. Synoptic weather map, 22 August.

carts that heaved their loads along the tracks to Killala during another dry and balmy night.

Could the favourable weather last? To the south of Cork a depression was hovering. As yet it was having no effect on Irish weather. But if it tracked northwards and brought a change of weather to the west, it would be a blow to Humbert as he tried to establish a foothold and set the west ablaze. He needed the good weather to last a while longer.

23-24 AUGUST: THE FALL OF BALLINA

The threat from the weather receded as the depression moved away to the east towards England and the atmospheric pressure rose rapidly across Ireland.[16] This growing ridge of high pressure produced another sunny, warm day in Mayo, although the temperatures were slightly lower due to the wind on the northern edge of the anticyclone becoming westerly (Fig 5.6). But this would not be felt in the shelter of Killala Bay and the lowlands of the Moy River, where the weather, at least, must have made the French feel almost at home.

The French needed to make quick progress, establish their command over the region and prepare for an advance across Ireland. The first step was to capture Castlebar. An early morning reconnaissance along the River Moy confirmed that there was a garrison at Ballina blocking their way. It was decided on a night attack for which the dry, clear weather was ideal. At 11pm, a force of 500 French and Irish led by French officers set out.[17]

But refugees from Killala had alerted Ballina. The fine night also provided excellent conditions for the Ballina cavalry to probe for intelligence. About 400 of them unexpectedly encountered the advancing French and fled. Back in Ballina it was decided to take the offensive. In an all-or-nothing strategy the entire garrison advanced under the cover of darkness. This progressed until attacked by Sarrazin near Rosserk Abbey. The fighting was deadlocked for some time. To break this, Sarrazin ordered a flank attack by an Irish company. In the darkness this unexpectedly gave an impression that a new, rear attack was being made. There was a confused, uncertain response that turned quickly into an unco-ordinated retreat. In the darkness the Ballina garrison had gained little idea of the size of the enemy force so, before sunrise, the entire garrison was evacuated to Foxford, a much more defensible point some ten miles away.

Despite the good weather the night was very dark. It was either moonless or perhaps even cloudy. In the blackness of the night unfamiliarity with the drumlin terrain of small hills and boggy depressions gave the French some difficulty with their bearings as they meandered between them. To assist them the residents who lived along the track they were using marked out the road by burning straw torches. The road is still known today as Bothar na sop (Road of the straw).[18]

The success of the battle for Ballina, following on from the capture of Killala, brought many new recruits from the countryside around. It has been estimated that between 600 and 700 men joined up. These

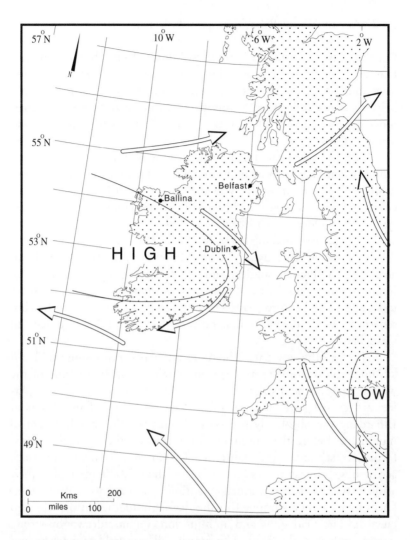

Fig 5.6. Synoptic weather map, 23 August.

were armed and clothed by the French but, critically, were given little or no drilling or training because time was too short. Although the French considered these recruits as being of very little military value, they did provide the benefit of creating an impression that the force was more formidable than really was the case.

26-27 AUGUST: SURPRISE ROUTE TO CASTLEBAR

On Saturday 25 August, a local priest informed Humbert of a mountain track that would bring him to Castlebar from an unexpected direction.[19] This was just what Humbert wanted, since surprise would help offset the imbalance of numbers. He decided on another night move. It was bold and adventurous. But it did not work. In fact it was nearly a disaster.

A low pressure system had threatened the weather but moved away rapidly when high pressure built up again. In fact, now the pressure was nearly as high as during the Wexford rising. A clockwise anticyclonic circulation was soon well established with light winds. But the pressure system was so located that the air circulation brought warm air off the sea from the west, making it very moist, and thundery (Fig 5.7).

At 4pm on 26 August General Humbert left Ballina with his artillery, 800 French soldiers and 1,500 local recruits. To give the impression of using the usual route to Castlebar, he marched for some miles along the Foxford road. Then he turned to the west to the chosen route, while the news that he was heading for Foxford sped to Castlebar.

That was the easy part. The route was across peaty soils and blanket bog, culminating in a craggy mountain track. It was one of the wildest parts of the district.[20] The first part of the march was straightforward crossing wet mineral soils. Even so, a rest of two hours at Lahardane was absolutely necessary. Thereafter, the march became a nightmare. Before the mountains were reached the night was transformed by thunder and lightning. Torrential rain made the track across bogs almost impassable as more than 2,000 men plus their artillery turned it into a morass. At times the men were up to their knees in it as they stumbled in the dark, blundering into rocks and crevices. The field guns and ammunition wagons, drawn by strong horses, sank into the mud. The carriage of one field gun broke and valuable time was lost with repairs. The horses could not cope and men had to take their place.[21] It was already dawn when Humbert's men reached the rocky mountain pass of Barnageehy ('windy gap'). If hope of a surprise attack lessened with the dawn, it sank without trace when a yeoman visiting his farm saw the column in the pass and galloped away with the news.

The French-Irish force descended to a ridge overlooking Castlebar. There, at about 6am, a very thick morning mist was rapidly dispersed by the sun and General Humbert saw in the clear morning light

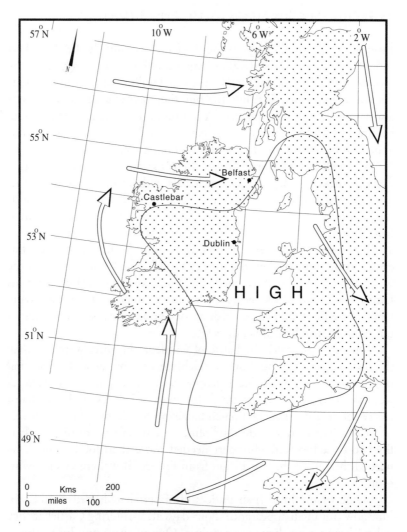

Fig 5.7. Synoptic weather map, 26 August.

General Hutchinson's force taking up positions below.[22] Overnight the weather had given the advantage to his enemy. But the British forces,in positions of their own choosing, proved unable to benefit from facing a tired enemy even after receiving advance warning of the French. In a series of bold moves which broke the cohesion of Castlebar's defenders, the French-Irish force caused panic among the infantry, silenced the artillery and put the entire British force to flight. It was a most remarkable victory against all the odds.

Everything appeared to favour the French. It is unlikely that Humbert thought much about the weather, even though the night trek across the mountains had been so difficult. He was familiar with summer thunderstorms in France, just like the one they had encountered. He was also familiar with protracted spells of fine summer weather that would be broken briefly from time to time. Clearly, the weather did not appear to be a cause for alarm, and no doubt everyone was glad of it.

Meanwhile, the British frigate *Cerberus* was off the Isle of Aran. Over the next two days it sailed to Killala with a small squadron. In its log it recorded easterly breezes and light variable winds. These winds were pushing out from the high pressure centre that had now drifted from Ireland to Britain (Fig 5.8). The weather even seemed to encourage a strange contentment, not merely among Franco-Irish force, but even among some of their opponents as well. The landed gentry in the west should have felt threatened. But Lord Kilmaine, fishing with his family on Lough Mask, noted in his diary 'Report of French having landed at Killala confirmed. Fish all day-good sport. Kill one pike of ten pounds and three small ones'![23]

On the night after the battle of Castlebar bonfires were lit on all the high ground around, both to celebrate a victory as well as the vital purpose of encouraging local people to rise and join the French. A week of 'extremely hot weather' followed.[24] But even this did not entice the recruits that the French had expected. Some of the Irish volunteers began to resent the discipline and superior attitudes of their liberators.[25] However, Humbert needed more than local recruits, he needed the rest of the expedition from France. But there was no word of it.

Some of the local Irish leaders Humbert had hoped would join him now put in an appearance. Four days after entering Castlebar they helped him set up their first republic. One of these was John Moore who was appointed President of a twelve-member executive, and the provisional government of Connaght was declared on 31 August.[26] The new Irish leaders celebrated. But all this collapsed as soon as the French moved on.[27]

Throughout this time the Irish who had travelled with Humbert, and Bartholomew Teeling in particular, urged him to press forward to link up with other insurgent groups across Ireland.[28] They knew of the forces now moving against them. Cornwallis was making the most of the good weather and the mobility it afforded. But perhaps none of

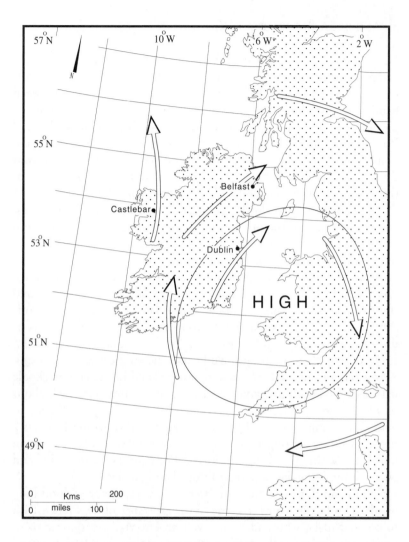

Fig 5.8. Synoptic weather map, 28 August.

Humbert's officers knew the type of country ahead of them and how difficult crossing it might be in poor weather. While bathed in sunshine such problems seemed remote. The French were to discover how unstable and fickle Irish weather could be, even in summer. Even the Irish with Humbert were only familiar with summers elsewhere in Ireland and may have had little idea of how wet the west could become and its effect on the tracks they would have to use.

30 AUGUST: A BLOCKADE FOR KILLALA

On a calm, clear morning the inhabitants of Killala woke to find they had new visitors. This time it was the British frigate *Cerberus* and the cutter *Hurler*. They entered Killala Bay knowing the town to be in French hands. The town had been under observation from a distance during the previous two days by a squadron of five British ships in Donegal Bay.[29] Peering at them on the far horizon watchers in Killala (especially the French garrison of 200 men left by Humbert) had hopes that this was the second French squadron from Brest. But just after dawn only two of them were left as the remainder disappeared towards Sligo.

At 6am these two slowly approached in a light north-north-east wind. This was not the product of a land-sea breeze since it was too early in the day for one to develop. Instead, it was the random result of slack winds right across the north of Ireland, due to the nearby anticyclone (Fig 5.9). Killala harbour is well protected from an attack directly from the sea. The approach is too shallow for frigate-sized ships to manoeuvre and a sand bar and isolated rocks are further offshore hazards. These could only be countered in specific weather conditions. Remarkably, these now prevailed. The light winds and calm sea favoured an action using small boats. The attack began at 7.30am. All the boats from the *Cerberus* were lowered and Lieutenant Stackpole led a party to attack two sloops that were either already in the harbour or which were approaching it.[30] One had been used by the French to land their ammunition and the other had a load of oatmeal. It was a fierce encounter lasting two hours. There were several casualties on both sides, including Stackpole himself. Both boats were set on fire and burnt through the day, and later lit up the night sky.

But conditions close to shore were tricky, especially with onshore winds. This fact was now to come to the assistance of the French-Irish forces in Killala, who had been given an effective demonstration of their vulnerability. As the morning progressed the winds freshened and the *Hurler* got into difficulties before going aground on a sand bar. At 10am a launch had to be sent from the *Cerberus* to help it. Over the next two days all the efforts of the *Cerberus* went into saving the cutter. Long hours were spent baling and pumping and removing its guns to lighten the ship. Occasionally the *Cerberus* fired towards the shore, especially when they saw activity in the harbour, discouraging any temptation to interfere. However, on one occasion it was merely townspeople scavenging on the oatmeal sloop that narrowly escaped death from an eighteen pounder. Both the *Cerberus* and the *Hurler*

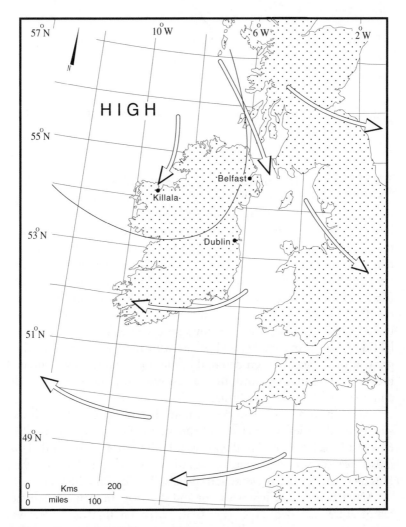

Fig 5.9. Synoptic weather map, 30 August.

could be thankful that there was no artillery on shore for they would have been sitting targets. Finally, on 2 September the struggle succeeded and the cutter was refloated. The following morning the *Fox* arrived and took the *Hurler* in tow and, with the assistance of some crew from the *Cerberus*, took the boat to Killybegs.

6

SEPTEMBER: THE HARVEST IN THE WEST

Where were the French reinforcements and where was the Irish support? Connaght had been peaceful all summer, so few troops were there.[1] Historians have wondered why relatively few Irish joined Humbert. Perhaps the weather was *too good*.[2] Knowing its fickleness the priority was to harvest while it was dry. Right across Ireland the harvest had started and many were reluctant to leave it and risk a hungry year. Even yeomen and militias wanted to return to their harvest.[3] Mr Little, rector of Lacken, wrote: '... the cattle had broken into the cornfields or were driven there and were feeding on or treading down the corn; some parts of the meadows remained as the grass had been laid down from the scythe, and others with the hay left in foresaken grasscocks; the flax was left deserted in the stooks until it was scorched brown by the sun; in a word, the harvest was left to take care of itself, and every field proclaimed future famine.'[4]

Many histories of these events note that the fine weather broke when Humbert left Castlebar (3 September). But anticyclonic influences had weakened before then (Fig 6.1). Rain had occurred daily in most areas except the west and south coasts (Fig 6.2). So, when Humbert left Castlebar *in* the rain, he also headed *into* the rain.

On 1 September, it was so hot and dry that the Armagh midday temperature exceeded 21⁰C (Fig 6.3).[5] Even on that day there was already heavy rain in south County Mayo.[6] Thereafter, the weather deteriorated as a succession of depressions brought more wind and rain.

During the month there were three remarkable journeys. The first was by Humbert from the west into central Ireland. This was constrained all along by the breaking weather. Secondly, Napper Tandy's relief expedition from France in the *Anacreon,* which was made possible largely by the opportune timing of favourable weather. Finally, the invasion fleet from Brest headed for Ireland, when allowed by the weather, but was shadowed and harried all the way by British frigates.

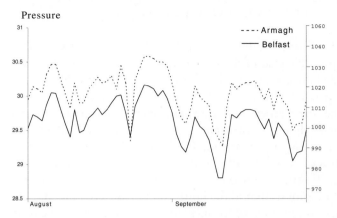

Fig 6.1. Daily pressure at Armagh and Belfast, August and September, 1798.

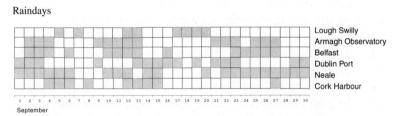

Fig 6.2. Raindays across Ireland in September.

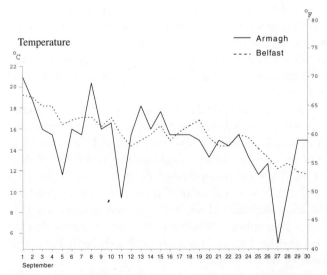

Fig 6.3. Daily midday temperatures at Armagh and Belfast in September.

3 SEPTEMBER: THE FRENCH LEAVE CASTLEBAR

The spell of brilliant weather ended before the French left Castlebar. They were probably glad of the shelter the town provided when heavy rain descended throughout the day. The weather register at Neale gives a picture of persistent heavy rain that became even heavier in the afternoon. While the French and Irish probably sheltered, Cornwallis marched for six hours in the pouring rain to camp at Hollymount, which was only about ten miles from Castlebar.[7] The net was closing in.

The depression responsible for this was much deeper than many that summer. In Armagh the pressure had plunged to 980 mbs and the central low pressure further to the north would have been much deeper (Fig 6.4). It is not unusual for such an intense storm to arrive from across the Atlantic at the end of an Irish summer. In the night the rain eased after the cold front had passed through, but the wind became very strong, driving the now showery rain before it.[8] But a warm front heralding the next depression was not far behind (Fig 6.4).

Humbert had three options. Firstly, to remain and fight the much larger force of Cornwallis. This seemed an unnecessary risk without further French or Irish reinforcements. Secondly, to march to where the United Irishmen were organised in the north or the midlands. With the possibility that his force would swell significantly, this had considerable attraction. Thirdly, since he expected the arrival of the Brest expedition any day, to wait for them in the mountains. But knowing they would first try to land in Donegal, and that British ships were already in Donegal Bay, it was clear that the two French groups would have a hard time meeting up. The second option seemed to be the best, especially when news arrived that Counties Sligo and Leitrim had only small garrisons. The Irish leaders with Humbert had urged this policy for some days.

But when did the Franco-Irish army leave Castlebar? Accounts vary between 3 and 4 September. If half left late on 3 September and the remainder before dawn the next day, they may well have been taking advantage of an easing in the torrential rain that had fallen all day.[9] Accounts that they left on 4 September do not fit with the vivid descriptions of the rain, as it was a day of spasmodic showers, and this is probably the incorrect date. Moore's diary is very precise and gives the morning of 3 September.[10] Whatever the truth, it seems that the rain arrived before the French departure and may well have contributed to the final hours of delay.

When Cornwallis' forces arrived at a late hour, it was still pouring

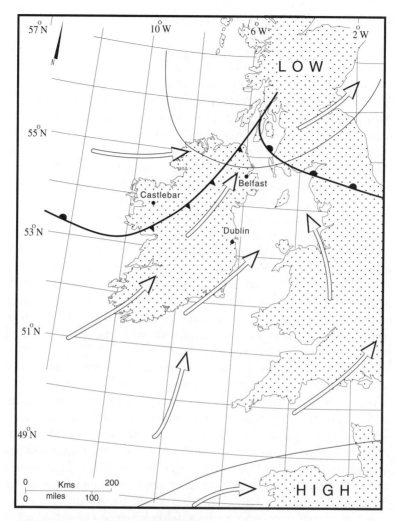

Fig 6.4. Synoptic weather map, 3 September.

with rain.[11] The French marched on without taking shelter, to get ahead of the pursuit. Although they rested at Swinford they pushed on to make their first camp at Bellaghy after 25 miles in conditions that must have appeared to be as wet underfoot as the skies above them. Although not as bad as the night march before the battle of Castlebar, even Humbert's hardened troops would have found it exhausting to trek at speed across the heavy gley soils and peat bogs on narrow roads, but there was much more of that ahead.[12]

4 September: A Lone Relief Expedition

The fastest corvette in the French navy, the *Anacreon*, loaded with supplies, guns and ammunition, had been waiting at Dunkirk for favourable weather to sail to Ireland. The route selected for this adventure by its Irish leader, Napper Tandy, was northwards across the North Sea and around the coast of Scotland. This was an unlikely route. It was at least 300 miles longer and passed through stormier waters than the normal westerly route. But it would avoid most British ships deployed around the Irish coast and achieve the benefit of surprise. Hence the necessity of waiting in Dunkirk for a suitable southerly or south-westerly wind to implement the plan. A growing anticyclone over Holland created the opportunity for the *Anacreon* to race away on the journey of its life (Fig 6.5).

Since 24 August over northern France the winds had been mostly easterly or northerly. East winds would drive them into the Channel, with little chance of avoiding the British fleet. With northerly winds rapid headway would be difficult. Speed was the particular advantage of the *Anacreon* and it was important to use it to the full. To sail in wind conditions that made progress both slow and difficult would expose them to discovery and capture.

The North Sea was dominated by the British navy. There were a series of naval ports along the east coast of England. From the Downes in the southeast to Yarmouth in the east and even as far north as Leith in Scotland, the navy was strategically placed, sometimes to protect fisheries, or to gather convoys together or otherwise for being victualled before leaving on service. Regular convoys crossed the North Sea to places as far afield as Hamburg, Bergen and the Baltic. Thus a route along the eastern side of the North Sea was no guarantee of avoiding detection. However, a fast, single ship would be of little interest to ships on convoy duty, whose duties did not permit chasing prizes in any case.[13] But the patrols off the north French coast still made it difficult to leave a Channel port. The frigate *Ariadne* was stationed off Calais while the *Dart* was patrolling between Ostend and Calais.

Once loaded and ready, the *Anacreon* waited. On 2 September the weather began to change as the pressure rose on the continent to the south. This ensured that the rapidly moving Atlantic depression that arrived over Ireland on 4 September followed its predecessor of the previous day northeastwards. However, along the North Sea coast of France light offshore breezes developed in response to the large-scale pressure gradients (Fig 6.5). The *Dart* remained just over the western

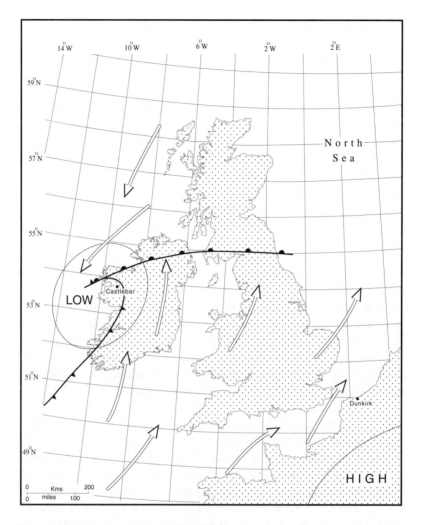

Fig 6.5. Synoptic weather map, 4 September.

horizon, but the *Ariadne* decided 'to look into Dunkirk', and arrived the next day.[14] But their new station became uncomfortable as thunderstorms developed, followed on 4 September by fresh gales from the southwest. These drove off the *Ariadne* and in poor weather it did not see the *Anacreon* slip away at 4pm.[15] The wind returned to northerly three days later, and the *Ariadne* stayed close to Dunkirk for another week. The corvette had been given an ideal start to its journey.

5 SEPTEMBER: THE BATTLE OF COLLOONEY

The depression that had broken the good weather and brought so much rain to Ireland moved on quickly towards Scotland and was followed by yet another on 4 September that produced widespread showery weather (Fig 6.5). By the following day this had also moved away (Fig. 6.6) to be replaced by blustery, colder weather. The tropical air enjoyed for so long was now replaced by air from polar regions and the temperatures dropped rapidly. In Armagh and Belfast midday temperatures became 6-7°C cooler. Strong winds remained along the coast, but they were moderate on land.

As the French and Irish dried out, they resumed their march in the early morning of 5 September towards Tubbercurry. There, the vanguard was attacked by a regiment of cavalry from Sligo. Having lost two officers and had prisoners taken, they fled back to the town. Although some accounts claim that there was a steady trickle of desertions from this point onwards, it is clear that new recruits also arrived. Parts of the west continued to have very heavy rainfall during the morning and the importance of several days of forced marching in suddenly colder, wet weather should not be underestimated as a factor in these desertions. However, the determination of a large group to join Humbert from Ballina and crossed the Ox Mountains during the appalling weather would have been of some cheer.[16]

The Franco-Irish force advanced to Collooney. Here Colonel Vereker, with a detachment of Limerick militia, had taken up a position between the river on his left and a series of rocky hills on his right in order to oppose their progress. Humbert's army made a frontal attack along the lower ground against Vereker's positions. But they made very slow progress and fighting was very severe. An unexpected opportunity arose when Humbert was given local information about a small valley on his left, of which he was unaware. As a result he was able to carry out a flanking move behind the hill on Vereker's right that was not observed until it was too late. The attack broke Vereker's force, which retreated. Their abandoned guns and stores became a most welcome prize.[17]

Much criticism has been levelled at Vereker for failing to cover the hills on his right flank. This lapse seems strange given the obvious respect that even Humbert had for Vereker's military capability.[18] Perhaps the hills did not appear to pose a strategic threat. If so, the weather probably helped to give this impression. The weather that day was very poor. Further south in County Mayo there was very heavy

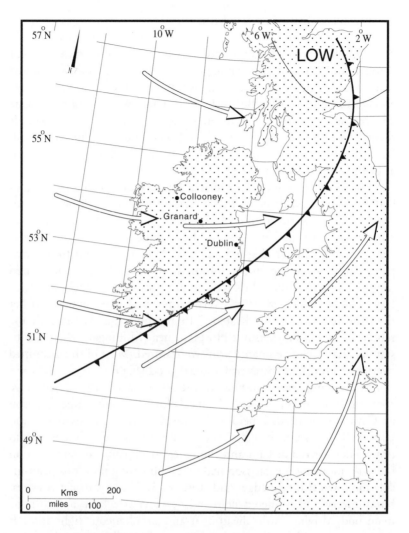

Fig 6.6. Synoptic weather map, 5 September.

rain that was only to clear later as the cold front moved away. In the north the Armagh register recorded a very 'overcast morning, damp and threatening rain'.[19] Nearby in Donegal Bay strong gales and squalls of rain were logged.[20] To Vereker, the clouds were low, threatening and wind-driven over hills that were saturated from the rain of the past few days. The hills would seem a most unlikely direction from which the French would launch an attack.

5 September: Risings in the Midlands

News of the French landing and subsequent successes caused a stir throughout the country. In some places the United Irishmen hesitated to act because there was uncertainty whether the French force was large enough to be successful. But in Longford and Westmeath they made contact with Humbert and encouraged him to head towards them.[21] They also decided to create a diversion by attacking Granard. Its fortified barrack would be useful for the advance on Dublin as well as being a supply of arms.

Both the depressions responsible for so much of the recent rain had moved in a north-north-east direction. After the belt of rain associated with the warm front of 4 September had passed over, there was a much greater time lapse than in the west before the following cold front arrived (compare Fig 6.5 and 6.6). When the warm front's rain petered out on 4 September hundreds of United Irishmen poured towards Granard from all directions and camped that night at Fruen Hill. The warm sector air was very humid and it felt much warmer than the temperatures indicated.[22] In neighbouring Westmeath the rebels converged on Wilson's Hospital, near Mullingar, where a substantial quantity of yeomanry arms were stored. Most of them camped overnight a few miles away at Crookedwood (Fig 6.7).

In Granard's garrison, news of the rebel movements caused grave concern. From midnight several appeals for help to the larger garrison at Cavan were needed before the threat was taken seriously and Captain Cottingham brought 100 cavalry to its aid.[23] It was just in time. They arrived at 8am and the rebel attack came at 9am.[24] From the early morning the garrison had taken up strong positions just outside the town behind hedges and stone walls. The weather was warm, but showery and hindered neither side. The attack began with the main body driving cattle ahead of it and simultaneous right and left flanking attacks. This forced the defenders to pull back to the town. And then the main belt of rain that marked the passage of the front arrived (Fig 6.6). The cold front that had been tracking slowly across the country crossed the area in the late morning bringing bursts of heavy cold rain. As the fighting spread into the town the rebels became fragmented. In the fighting, the loss of key rebel leaders led to uncertainty, some confusion and then a retreat. By this time the rain had passed, the temperatures had fallen and the insurgents were wet, cold and leaderless. This opportunity was immediately seized by the cavalry which, using the relatively open ground, charged and routed the

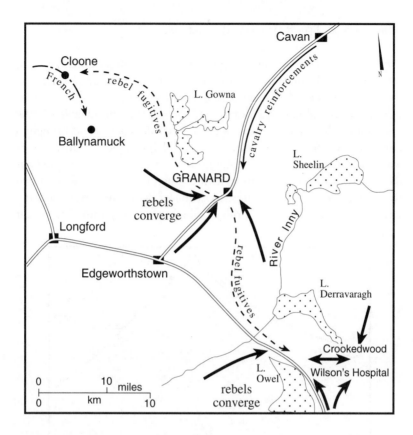

Fig 6.7. The attack on Granard.

attackers with considerable loss of life. The battle had lasted five hours, but the slaughter continued in the cornfields as the rebels fled.

At Wilson's Hospital the rebels had returned in the morning from their night quarters and, with little opposition, they made the building their headquarters. Crookedwood still remained the camp for the main body of insurgents and it received a surge of newcomers that night as fugitives from the reverse at Granard arrived for sanctuary and to re-group. Their own confrontation with government forces came the next day.

Many of those who fled from Granard headed towards the advancing army of Humbert. Because of the pursuit, this was not easy. However, they met up on 7 September at Cloone. The news of the defeat at Granard, and more particularly the loss of a large additional fighting force, dashed Humbert's hopes that his strategy might work.

6 SEPTEMBER: THE BATTLE OF BUNBRUSNA

Fresh from their victory, 600 infantry and artillery under Lord Longford were dispatched from Granard to Bunbrusna, and took up positions on the high road. They had every reason to be cautious. The rebel numbers were unknown, although a local source had put their number at 10,000.

During the early morning hours another depression had brought a fairly weak warm front across the country. While it yielded little rain, it was much more effective in bringing back warm air. After the previous day, the warmer air was most welcome. The midlands lay between two weather influences. To the north a string of depressions were crossing Ireland while to the south a ridge of high pressure pumped warm air

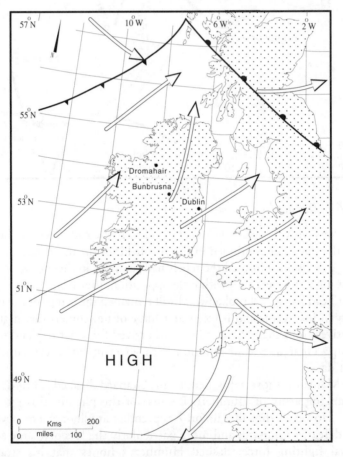

Fig 6.8. Synoptic weather map, 6 September.

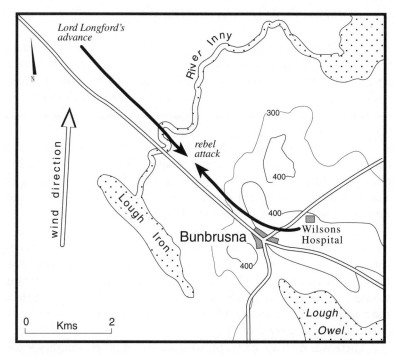

Fig 6.10. Barden's attack on Lord Longford's force.

towards it. As a result, bands of cloud marked the fronts rather than rain.

The rebels at Wilson's Hospital heard about Longford's deployment and a large group led by Christopher Barden, buoyed by the arms they had acquired from the armoury attacked their enemy. They made a frontal attack that was tactically naïve and losses were high. The rebels' attempt to overwhelm Longford by their numerical advantage was dashed by artillery fire and then the deployment of cavalry.

The weather played a small, but not decisive, role in this battle. Longford had taken up positions facing southwards, the road being aligned northwest-southeast (Fig 6.9). The wind blew in the direction of the rebels' attack. This readily dispersed the artillery smoke behind Longford's lines rather than drifting and thickening ahead of the guns. Consequently, the attacking rebels could not have been easier targets and their frontal attack made their losses high.

Broken as a force, the rebels defended themselves as best they could until darkness fell. Many fell back to Wilson's Hospital and their main force. There, in the early hours of 7 September, it was decided to discontinue the fight and they used the darkness of another cloudy night to escape onto the islands and rush beds of the River Inny and its loughs.[25]

6-7 September: From Drumlin to Drumlin

After Coolloney, Humbert turned eastwards and soon entered drumlin country. This is particularly fatiguing and sometimes bewildering landscape to march through. Its small convex hills have sharp slopes with tracts of wet, marshy ground in between – with few short cuts! So the roads were narrow and meandering with varying gradients that at times seem to lead nowhere.

Cornwallis sent Lake to harry Humbert's force. In fact, such a landscape gave few opportunities to spread out for a pitched battle. But Humbert still tried to gain an advantage at the northward turning to Manorhamilton. He posted his vanguard there to make Lake's scouts think they were headed northwards. Then he marched southwards.[26]

The next day, 7 September, the River Shannon was reached and crossed at Ballintra. The mountains disappeared behind them as they entered a much denser drumlin landscape, with fewer distant landmarks to mark their progress. To the south Cornwallis was marching to stop Humbert linking with the midland rebels and cut him off from the capital. Marching round the drumlins, Humbert was not easily visible, especially at a distance (Fig 6.10).

There was no help for Humbert from the weather. Another warm front arrived from the west, but even as far north as Armagh it only produced cloud during the morning (Fig 6.11). There was little rain anywhere. Even that would hardly slow up the larger forces following

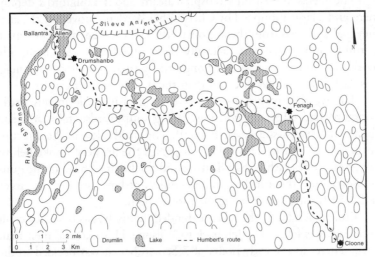

Fig 6.10. Humbert's route across the drumlin country between Drumshanbo and Cloone.

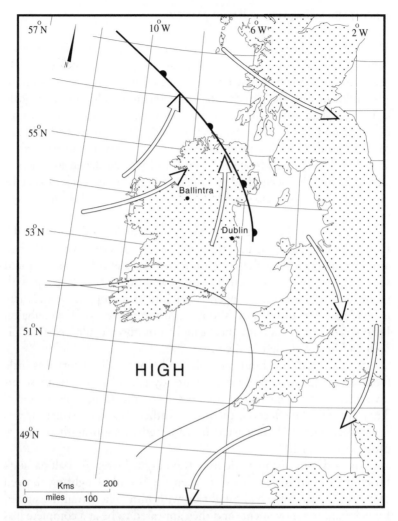

Fig 6.11. Synoptic weather map, 7 September.

him. Speed was what Humbert needed and had the ground been drier and more negotiable he might have achieved this. The weather and the terrain had combined against him to slow him down and exhaust his troops. That night Humbert ordered a brief night stop at Cloone. It has often been argued that had Humbert carried straight on, Cornwallis would have failed to intercept him, and had they got seven miles further into County Longford they would have been joined by thousands of reinforcements, 'and the campaign would have assumed a new character'.[27] But they had little choice: they needed to rest.

8 September: Battle of Ballinamuck

The impact of the weather and the terrain on great endeavours is often cumulative, and so it was with the final act of Humbert's campaign. By the time the French reached Ballinamuck, they had marched about 110 miles in four days under the most trying conditions, with little rest. They had marched through rainstorms and across a tortuous boggy terrain. Even when there was no rain, the 'marshy and difficult roads' it produced still slowed them down and sapped their strength.[28] The Irish lacked the French discipline and war-hardened experience, and more readily succumbed to fatigue. On dropping back or snatching some sleep, their pursuers found many of them and showed them no mercy.

Apart from the physical exhaustion, the determination of the French was being weakened from within. After Castlebar some had already concluded that the expedition was futile and Humbert should surrender. As more Irish slipped away or struggled to keep up with them their case became stronger. At each further stopping point there is evidence of dissension about continuing, as at Dromahaire, Drumkeeran and Cloone. Increasingly Humbert could see that his men had little fight left in them.

Similar hardships hindered Lake and Cornwallis. There was little food or rest. Lake found most food already taken by the French so his own men were often taking potatoes from the fields they passed.[29] They also felt the effects of the poor weather. But their situation was never desperate and they were transformed as soon as their quarry came within reach.[30]

Many details of the battle have been argued over. At Ballinamuck Humbert turned to face his rear when the sound of fighting showed that Lake's main force had caught up with him. The terrain frustrated French flanking movements and they appeared to be at a complete loss to understand the deceptive nature of the marshy low-lying ground. In one instance they advanced onto a marsh with a surface as hard as a meadow only to find themselves sinking up to their waists.[31] In another they had to leap across hummocks to avoid sinking into the mud.[32] It was a short day for the French who surrendered after a brief fight and who, as prisoners of war, were given quarter. But it was a very long day for the Irish who expected no quarter and had to fight their way out. The bogs and hills gave a little hope as they fled and there are many stories of narrow escapes.[33] But large numbers were killed where they were cornered, fighting a desperate retreat and fleeing through bogs

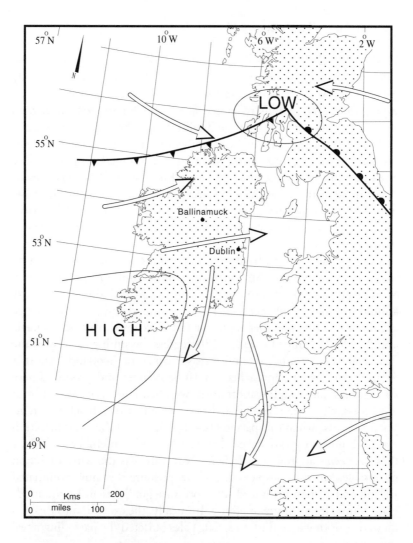

Fig 6.12. Synoptic weather map, 8 September.

and ditches.

If the weather had been of little help in their march across Roscommon and Leitrim, it came to the help of many survivors now, at least for the next two days. Until 10 September warm humid air continued to arrive from the southwest to produce cloudy, warm days and nights and at times it was sunny and fine (Fig 6.12). Most of the rebels had to hide by day and travel by night, as they headed westwards back to their homes in County Mayo.

12 SEPTEMBER: FAVOURABLE WINDS

Having left Dunkirk on 4 September with a following wind, the *Anacreon* made rapid progress in the first 24 hours. It successfully passed the east coast of England where the chances of being spotted were greatest. The winds remained favourable for the first three days (Fig 6.13). It is probable that the English frigate *Belliqueux* spotted the *Anacreon* on the morning of 7 September off the east coast of Scotland, since the latter's log records the sighting of a strange sail in almost the exact position where the *Anacreon* would have been.[34] But the weather was quite disturbed as the wind strengthened and veered to the west-north-west and rain restricted visibility. In any case, the *Belliqueux*'s responsibility was to the convoy it was escorting to Leith. So there was no pursuit.

At this point it must have appeared that the weather was beginning to change for the worse. Strengthening winds from north of west on 7 September seemed to promise a very rough and difficult passage around the north of Scotland. But a remarkably timely change occurred. On 8 September high pressure developed over Scandinavia and the winds changed through 180 degrees, becoming easterly as the *Anacreon* sailed round the north-east corner of Scotland. Another Atlantic depression approached on 10 September and produced very strong winds and rough seas off north-west Scotland. This was far from ideal for such a small, heavily-laden vessel. But this setback was temporary because when this passed (10-11 September) the wind direction veered to northerly and stayed that way until 12 September – ideal for the *Anacreon*'s approach to Ireland. Not only was the wind direction favourable, but the complex area of low pressure that now dominated Ireland and Britain produced weak pressure gradients and quite moderate winds along *Anacreon*'s route. Ironically, the exception to this was far to the south where fresh to strong gales buffeted the patrolling naval squadrons.

However, the northern coast of Ireland was also patrolled. If the weather had been remarkably favourable to Tandy's expedition so far, he could not assume all his problems were over. This was immediately apparent during *Anacreon*'s first approach to the coast during the morning. About fifteen miles out two ships patrolling the entrances to Loughs Foyle and Swilly were spotted. Captain Blankmann turned the *Anacreon* about until they were safely out of sight. It is doubtful that they were spotted and a single sail would cause little alarm. As the *Anacreon* sailed further into the west later that day the winds picked

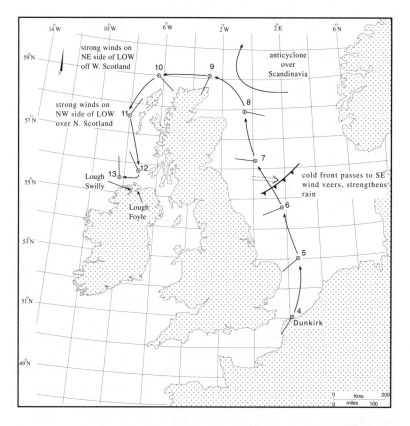

Fig 6.13. Weather along the Anacreon's *route bewteen Dunkirk and Donegal, September 1798 (dates, wind directions and synoptic features are shown).*

up, the sea became heavy and the night became very wet.

Ireland now lay over the horizon about 45 miles away. It was clear that a direct route would not be possible without encountering navy patrols, against whom they would be heavily outgunned. They needed a strategy that would maximise their own advantages of speed and surprise to make a landing, providing the weather allowed.

13 September: A Place to Land

Having sailed far to the west the *Anacreon* had succeeded in steering a wide berth of the frigates patrolling the north coast. Behind the cold front that had produced so much rain during the night the pressure began to rise quite rapidly and the cold air became very clear (Fig 6.14). By 9am they were north of Tory Island and for the first time in the sparkling clear air the mountains of Donegal came into view some twelve to fifteen miles away.[35] No other vessels were in sight. Even on land it was a beautiful, bright morning.[36]

The *Anacreon* had arrived in exceptionally good time. The wind and weather had been favourable throughout the journey resulting in not only a fast journey time but also in avoiding warships in the North Sea. Of the four expeditions from France to Ireland during 1798, this one had achieved the shortest journey time. The journey of over 1,000 miles to Donegal had taken only nine days (4–13 September) to reach Tory Island, although a further three passed before landing. The western route, used by the other expeditions, had taken Commodore Savary (from Rochefort) sixteen days, Bompard (from Brest) 21 days and Savary, on his final return visit, fifteen days. It was a remarkable achievement, due largely to the weather.

In the late afternoon when they were much closer to the coast, another ship appeared, this time from between Sheephaven and Tory Island. It was alone and proved to be the sloop *Swan*. This was an opportunity to gather information. While still at a distance, and to prevent the *Swan* becoming alarmed, the English colours were hoisted. As it did so, the *Anacreon* manoeuvred to the windward where it would have the strategic advantage in any action that might follow. That was easily done because the wind was already from the north. The strategy was completely successful and the *Swan* was taken. Tandy discovered that it was sailing from Lough Foyle to Galway. About Humbert, the captain, William Kelly, was only able to tell that the French were not in Donegal but had gone inland. Although further information was obtained on Humbert's progress, it does not appear to have included the surrender at Ballinamuck.[37] It was decided to keep Kelly on board to act as a pilot in the tricky western coastal waters.

By midnight the weather became dead calm and little progress could be made. At this stage the *Anacreon* was just over three miles from the shore. The nearest available port was Dunfanaghy, but being advised by Kelly that this was unsuitable for the *Anacreon*, Tandy decided to sail for the sheltered waters inshore of Aran Island. Tandy

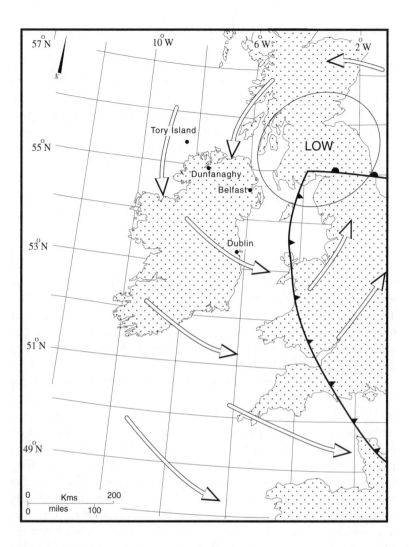

Fig 6.14. Synoptic weather map, 13 September.

was unaware that Killala was still held by the French and a large group of rebels. Undoubtedly that would have been his preferred destination had he known. Ignorance of this knowledge probably saved the *Anacreon* from the frigate *Cerberus*, which was patrolling further south in Donegal Bay because of the French in Killala. The following day the *Cerberus* was to sail westwards along the north Mayo coast and remain there for a few days.

16 September: The Sun Shines on Aran

Progress towards Aran was very slow. Having sailed so far in such a short time, it was ironic that the short distance from Tory Island to Aran Island (less than 25 miles) took over two days. The culprit was a strong wind that blew up from the west and became a severe gale requiring the *Anacreon* to keep a good distance from the coast. This developed into a severe eleven-hour storm that drove the ship far out to sea. After it died down Blankmann set course once again for the coast.

At 4am on Sunday 16 September Aran Island came into sight. In a slack southwesterly wind it took another six hours to reach the island. Flying English colours again the *Anacreon* signalled for a pilot (there was regular coastal trade along the coastline and pilots were available at Aran roads) who duly came out. By 11am the ship was anchored close to the shore since there was no deep-water berth. The morning had turned into a pleasant day with a growing ridge of high pressure off the south coast pushing warm breezes across most of Ireland (Fig 6.15). The fine weather drew some local people out in their curraghs, eager for a closer look. As they arrived, each was seized and questioned. But most were United Irishmen and soon they were as co-operative as Tandy could have wished.

Tandy decided to land to assess the extent of local support and his military options. To prevent any contact with the mainland he landed on Rutland Island (Inis Mhic a Duirn) where there was an important trading settlement. The post office was seized and he set a lookout on Aran's summit. This had views along the entire length of the west Donegal coast and would give a good early warning of patrolling frigates. Most local people welcomed the new arrivals. The Irish flag was raised and a proclamation issued calling for a war of liberty. Tandy learned the news of Humbert's defeat at Ballinamuck which was only just breaking in the area. But he was not entirely convinced. Since the post was brought out from Burtonport when the weather was favourable, as it was on this occasion, he hijacked it and checked for himself. It confirmed his fears. He reasoned that his force could do little by itself. Its main benefit would have been in joining with a larger one. There appeared to be no reason to stay.

The tradition that it was a beautiful harvest day, the corn cut and men sitting on stooks in the fields watching events develop is delightful, but probably of limited accuracy.[38] After a bright sunny morning, the north of Ireland generally was clouding over and was overcast throughout the remainder of the day, with a rising wind. Probably this

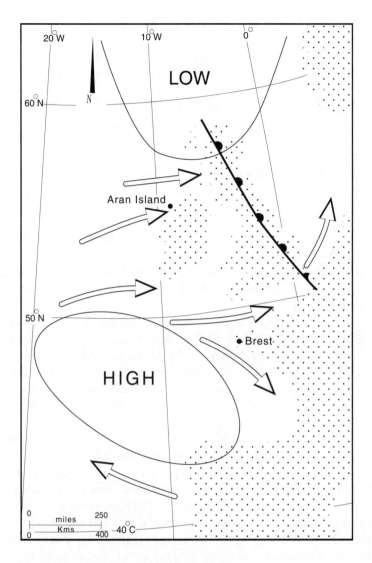

Fig 6.15. Synoptic weather map, 16 September.

is also what happened over Donegal as well. But it was still a reasonably pleasant autumn night as the French withdrew to the *Anacreon*,
the more enthusiastic islanders shouldering Tandy to his boat. But
postmaster Francis Foster, who was also the coast officer, had already
sent despatches to the military headquarters in Letterkenny warning
about the raid.

16 September: Wolfe Tone Finally Sets Sail

The French fleet in Brest under Bompard was still waiting to leave. Wolfe Tone's presence in the fleet, as well as their destination, was public knowledge both in France and in Britain. On the positive side the lengthy dispute with the French Ministry of the Marine over money to buy stores and pay the men had been resolved. Nevertheless, their departure was still delayed due to unfavourable winds and the blockade.[39]

The fleet waiting for a favourable wind consisted of just one ship of the line, the *Hoche (74 guns)*. But there were also seven frigates, the *Immortalite* and *Romaine* (both with 40 guns), the *Loire, Bellone, Coquille, Resolue* and *Semillante* (each with 36 guns) and finally a schooner, the *Biche*. Although this was a considerable amount of firepower it was intended to avoid the British and sail a long route westwards into the Atlantic to approach Ireland from the north or northwest, as Savary had done to take Humbert's expedition the previous month.[40]

At last the wind changed. Except for three days when the blockade had been too tight this was the first day of September when the wind had become easterly. For most of the day an anticyclone over the Bay of Biscay had resulted in westerlies from the Irish coast to France. But later in the day this drifted closer to Ireland and the winds over Brittany became easterly (compare Figs 6.15 and 6.17). The fleet was ready and put to sea.

Brest harbour is complex. The entrance to the inner harbour where the fleet assembled is narrow, called the goulet (neck of a bottle). This ensured both shelter and protection. Outside this the broad Iroise channel, at least fifteen miles wide, leads directly westwards (Fig 6.16). Occasionally a British frigate would advance into this to observe the inner harbour or even to attack a vessel that had ventured out. On the southern side of this channel the land tapers to the Pointe du Raz, the line of which can be traced offshore in the Illes de Sein. Between these is a narrow channel three to four kilometres wide, the Raz de Sein, providing an alternative exit, and the possibility of avoiding the watching eyes of the blockading fleet. However, this is a hazardous route with tricky coastal winds, particularly when numbers of ships are sailing together.

The fleet moved out of the harbour in the evening and headed through the Raz de Sein. The night was calm and bright as the fleet sailed carefully between the rocky outcrops – the same risky

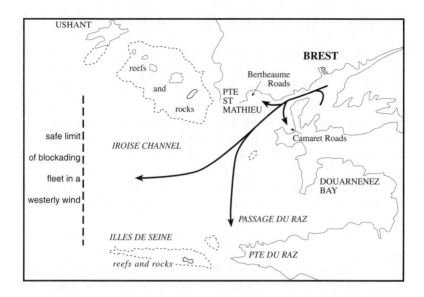

Fig 6.16. The exits from Brest harbour.

manoeuvre that had been used disastrously in 1796.[41] But this time it was carried out in an orderly manner without any loss of ships or loss of life. And what was most important of all, they were not seen. It was a timely tactical use of the new easterly wind that had temporarily pushed the blockading fleet further away.

In Ireland, Humbert and his officers were given a banquet in Longford town and then travelled to Dublin by canal. In a bright southerly airstream that brought out the crowds, their cavalcade entered the capital and for 24 hours they found 'the most delicate cares and attention' were lavished upon them 'as well as the most generous hospitality'.[42] Their war was over, even though others were trying to reach them to rekindle the flame that had all but gone out.

17 September: The Search for Tandy and Tone

Over Donegal the cloud thickened and the night was very dark. The *Anacreon* remained at its moorings until daybreak when it sailed off to the northeast. Initially it hugged the coastline to avoid detection before striking out into the open sea cutting across a south-westerly morning wind. The postmaster at Rutland Island sent a further despatch to Letterkenny to alert the navy in Lough Swilly. In the dry weather the messenger made excellent time through the mountains. However, his first message had already raised the alarm. At 2am the cavalry had set out for Burtonport and the Rosses while the infantry were due to follow at dawn. The cavalry met the second messenger, so they were alerted to the departure of the *Anacreon*.[43]

Meanwhile, in Lough Swilly, the frigates *Doris* and *Melampus* prepared to go after the *Anacreon,* but were delayed by a turn in the weather. The fine weather so enjoyed by Tandy the previous day was replaced by bands of rain and unfavourable winds. The south-west winds that had helped the *Anacreon*'s departure in the early morning now veered to the west and then the northwest as a cold front imposed itself over the coast (Fig 6.17). Eventually the frigates emerged from Lough Swilly at 7pm, nearly twelve hours after the reported departure of the *Anacreon* whose speed and the fortuitous timing of the weather made possible its escape. Had its departure been delayed it would have been difficult to get away from the coast, heading into the wind, and then escape the searching frigates. Instead, the few hours head start enabled it to take a route that bisected two converging threats. One was the advancing Lough Swilly squadron and the other was the *Cerberus* off the north Mayo coast that was patrolling towards Tory Island. Remarkably, neither the French nor the British caught sight of each other. Yet again the *Anacreon* had a charmed life. Veiled by the weather it slipped away as the frigates struggled through fresh gales, squalls and a curtain of rain, never sure where their enemy was to be found. Even so, Kingsmill in Cork expressed 'wonder and regret' at the escape.[44] But Tandy seized the benefit of the winds that now became westerly, strengthened and remained that way for several days. Conditions were so good for a rapid getaway that in two days the *Anacreon* was off the Orkneys. These came into view less than 48 hours after leaving Rutland Island having sailed more than 400 miles. Only then did the winds disrupt Tandy's plans, forcing him to Norway instead of going to France.

Meanwhile, off Brittany, the French had successfully negotiated

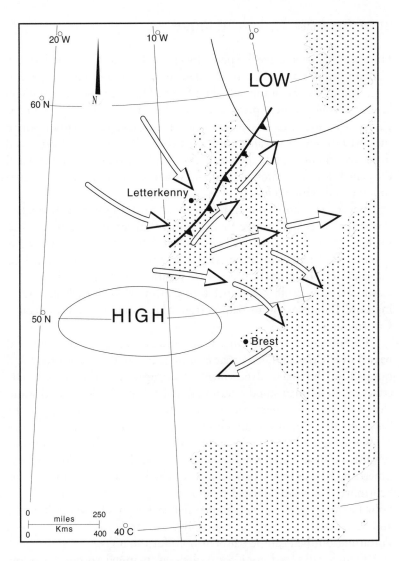

Fig 6.17. Synoptic weather map, 17 September.

the Raz de Sein during the night. But unlike the elusive Tandy, they were quickly spotted at dawn by the frigates *Boadicea* and *Ethalion* and the sloop *Sylph*. Almost calm conditions turned into a north-east breeze that the French used to sail to the south-south-west. The *Boadicea* set off to Plymouth with the news of the French break-out, while the others kept watch to see where they were going.[45] But the French wanted to throw off this most unwelcome 'tail'.

21-22 September: Retreat to Killala

Humbert had left three French officers in Killala, Colonel Charost, Captain Ponson and Captain Boudet, to guard the Protestant prisoners in the castle, the home of Bishop Stock. Humbert did not want any harm to come to these prisoners from the Irish insurgents. At times, particularly after the French garrison of 200 had been withdrawn to support Humbert's advance from Castlebar, Charost was hard-pressed to protect them. The French presence would also be important when the expedition from Brest arrived and when Savary returned with more supplies and reinforcements.

The news from Ballinamuck seemed to strengthen Irish resolve. Rather than seeking refuge in the hills an unsuccessful attempt was made to recapture Castlebar. These defeats and the stories of massacres renewed the anxiety of the prisoners at Killala. Stock secretly passed information about their precarious position to General Trench in Castlebar. As a result he advanced his plans to drive for Killala, ordering Lord Portarlington to Ballina from Sligo while he went to occupy Crossmolina.

Portarlington set out on 21 September after a warm front had passed over Connaght early that morning. He used the coast road and camped for the night at the village of Grange. Here they were briefly attacked, so his men stood to arms all night. But the night was dry and clear and gave no opportunity for the rebels to gain an advantage. The following day, Portarlington advanced along the east bank of the River Moy, leaving a trail of smoke and flame as his troops burned their way towards Ballina. Their progress was clearly visible from Killala on the other side of the bay, where it was watched with apprehension.[46] At Scurmore they were attacked by a force of pikemen. But after a hard hour-long engagement the pikemen fell back under heavy artillery fire and retreated to Ballina, skilfully covered by their cavalry. Portarlington then camped at Scurmore for the night.

Trench advanced to Crossmolina as planned, using the same mountain route through the Barnageehy Gap as Humbert a month earlier. When news of this reached Killala, Ferdinand O'Donnell led 300 men to reconnoitre and stop him. The night was pitch black as rain-clouds of an approaching cold front spread relentlessly from the southwest (Fig. 6.18). Soon it arrived and it took no time at all before the men were soaked. They trudged onwards into the blinding rain until a rest halt was called at Rappa Castle.[47] This may have been to take shelter as well as some liquor to counteract the fatigue of the rainy

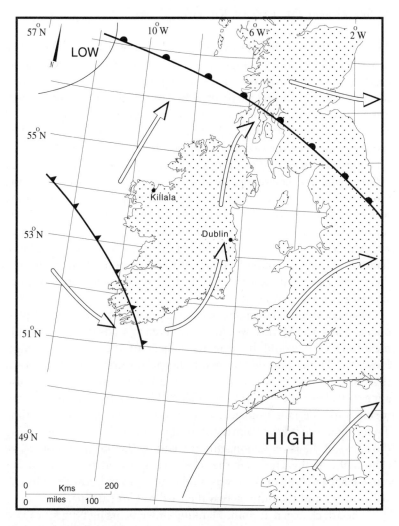

Fig 6.18. Synoptic weather map, 22 September.

march.[48] O'Donnell became ill and Roger McGuire took command. He took a small force to Crossmolina for reconnaissance but withdrew after a skirmish. In the dark and the rain it is unlikely that any idea of Trench's strength was gained. Visibility was poor and campfires were impossible. Although McGuire and O'Donnell returned to Killala because of the size of Trench's force, it is unlikely they had any clearer idea of its size than when they originally set out.

23 SEPTEMBER: THE FALL OF KILLALA

The day Killala finally fell can be divided into two distinct parts. The first was most of the morning, when the cold front passed slowly overhead and continued to produce rain (Fig 6.20). The overnight total was probably much greater than in Belfast where nearly half an inch was recorded.[49] But before noon the rain stopped, the clouds cleared and the sun shone brightly in a blustery wind from the south. The transition between the two was sharp, as often occurs with cold fronts.

Until the middle of the morning there were still opportunities to escape Nugent's encircling forces by heading westwards into the mountains. In the preceding days many had slipped home to get some of the harvesting done.[50] But most of the insurgents seemed determined to make a stand. Many had fallen back on Killala. Among those who withdrew to Killala was Captain Truc, the French commander of Ballina. The small group of French officers felt honour bound to join the rebels' last stand, at least in a token way, although they now considered the cause a futile one.

The continuing rain increased the anxiety of the Protestant prisoners. They feared this would delay Trench's advance and in the meantime they would become the object of the insurgents' rage. However, Trench was determined to keep his secret promise to Stock that he would be in Killala on Sunday 23 September. The rain also appears to have mesmerised the Irish.[51] They carried out no deployments until the rain stopped late in the morning. But by that time Trench had secured the Palmerston bridge and deployed his men along the banks of the River Cloonaghmore, closing the one means of escape (Fig 6.19). At this late stage the rebels set up two defensive positions outside Killala. One of these was on the high ground near the Moyne-Ballina road and the other across the road to Crossmolina.

The attack began at 3pm. Flanking movements by Nugent caused a retreat that became a rout when the cavalry charged the defenders. Fighting continued all afternoon, even into the night. Too late, fugitives found their retreat across Palmerston bridge blocked, the river full and strong after the recent rain and the tide too high to cross in Rathfran Bay. But some did break out southwards into the mountains.

Had the wind not veered from southerly to westerly as the cold front passed over Killala a catastrophe could have occurred. Ninety barrels of gunpowder had been buried in the garden of Bishop Stock to safeguard it. The troops entering Killala set fire to the cabins close-by, but the fresh winds behind the cold front drove the flames away

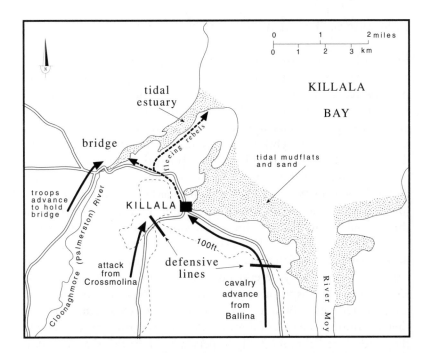

Fig 6.19. The fall of Killala, 23 September.

rather than engulfing the garden area. [52]

The weather came to the relief of the Mayo population in the ret-
ributions that followed. Rain, wind and storm became commonplace
for some weeks. In Killala the troops shivered in tents at the weather's
wetness and fury. Trench wanted to take his troops away and after they
had scoured the district, burnt cabins and pursued those 'rebels' they
could find, Trench withdrew to Castlebar on 30 September, leaving
only the Prince of Wales' fencibles at Killala to discourage any guerilla activity. Winter comes early in the northwest and already the
Atlantic gales were beating against Mayo's cliffs and mountains where
many of the refugees were still scattered, hiding in caves and bog-holes
and soon suffering from famine and exposure.[53]

23 SEPTEMBER: TO THE ANTILLES OR IRELAND?

In the Atlantic the British frigates shadowing Bompard's fleet still had a clear view of the French on 23 September. During the week that had passed since the French had left Brest on 16 September the wind had varied between calm and fresh. It had posed no problems to either group of ships. The task of Captain Countess in the frigate *Ethalion* had become very straightforward. He had to find out for certain the destination of the French and send the appropriate warnings.

At first the French had followed the coastline of Brittany eastwards and had manoeuvred as if to enter the port of Lorient. It was common for French ships to sail close to their coastline because of the constant threat from enemy ships.[54] But it was soon obvious to the following frigate that this was more than a coastal convoy because the ships were packed with troops. Whatever ploy the French may have used to conceal this fact initially, eventually they would have been seen by Countess and his suspicions confirmed. Seeing the British frigates were not persuaded and would not go away, the French chased them off and then continued to head southwards. Progress was slow, partly because the winds were light and partly to persuade the British that their destination was nowhere significant. Their course could take them further along the French coast or even out to the Antilles (West Indies). The longer they could keep a southerly course the less convinced the British would be that their destination was Ireland. Even with easterly winds, progress across the Bay of Biscay was slow.

The two British ships stayed a good distance away because the weather was so fine and they had little need to take the risks of getting close. But on 22 September the situation began to change. The winds had been moving around to the south, becoming favourable to Bompard for a dash northwards. Then on 23 September, with a southerly wind continuing, Countess brought his frigate close to the French, took a good look at their ships and decided to take the precaution of sending the *Sylph* to Ireland (Fig 6.20).[55] Plymouth had already been warned. Now Countess wanted to make sure that he used the southerly wind to warn Kingsmill at Cork of the potential threat, ahead of any French move in that direction.

On the same day the *Boadicea* arrived in Plymouth where it had been sent to advise Lord Bridport of the French moves. This was not unexpected because of the fairly public expectations of such a move in France. But now was the time for Bridport to respond. The same day a squadron under Sir John Warren in the *Canada* (a 74-gun ship of the

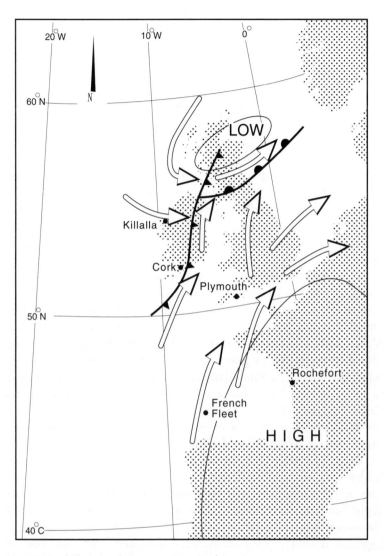

Fig 6.20. Synoptic weather map, 23 September.

line) left Plymouth for Ireland. Although the squadron was small, it was powerful. It consisted of another line of battle ship, the 80-gun *Foudroyant*, as well as the frigates *Robust* and *Magnanime*. They would join with other ships on the Irish station and be prepared in case the French had Ireland as their intended destination.

7

OCTOBER: THE FINAL STORM

The climax to 1798 was the return of Wolfe Tone to Ireland. He arrived with the largest of the expeditions from France. The delays that had frustrated it in Brest were compounded by the tortuous route it took to Ireland. Having sent the *Sylph* to warn Kingsmill, Countess on the *Ethalion* must have wondered. The French were still heading towards the southwest across the Bay of Biscay (Fig 7.1).

On 30 September they had reached latitude 43 degrees 50 minutes north, almost level with the north coast of Spain. But when they allowed a 100-ship convoy pass unmolested on 25 September, any likelihood that this was a squadron going to the Antilles was dispelled. Although their cover was blown, a direct course for Ireland was prevented by north-easterly gale force winds that blew for four days. The rough seas and severe winds damaged the ships and drove them further to the southwest. Even then the British frigates (the *Amelia* and the *Anson* had joined the *Ethalion*) shadowed them. The *Loire* and *Immortalite* failed to chase them away. Once Bompard had repaired the storm damage, he turned for Ireland.[1]

From 1 October his route was northwards aided by winds that varied between west and south-south-east (Fig 7.1). The weather became hazy and thickened as a gale blew up, during which the French suddenly found themselves free of their shadow. At last, with a sense that the enemy was not watching his every move, Bompard was able to approach Ireland as planned, from the northwest, with some hope of remaining unobserved. He aimed to land north of Killala where he expected Humbert to have advanced.

In the sea battle that followed later in the month there was a major action followed by a series of other engagements spread over seven days. Changing weather was used opportunistically in a number of instances. With some exaggeration the major action has been described, as 'one of the obstinate and desperate engagements which have ever been fought on the oceans' and 'a victory which, in its way, was as complete as

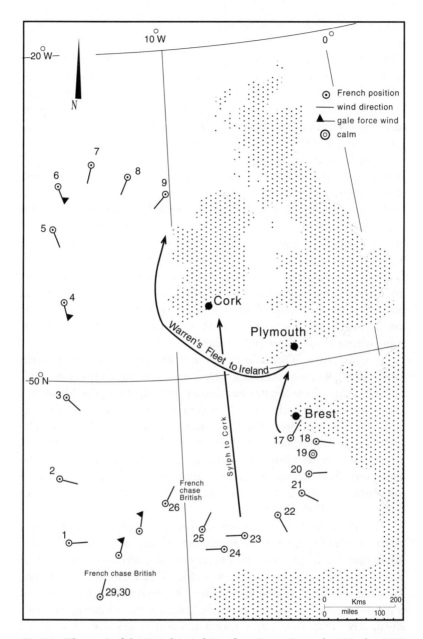

Fig 7.1. The route of the French expedition from Brest, September-October 1798 (dates, wind direction and gales are shown).

Nelson's', but there are no claims that it made a significant difference to the Irish cause.[2] The expedition arrived too late for that.

10 OCTOBER: DONEGAL IN SIGHT

A low pressure system brought a good spell of weather in early October to an end. The pressure gradient around the low was not severe, so at first the strength of the wind presented no problems to either the French or British fleets. But the logbook records show that the low pressure centre was close to the north coast of Ireland and wind directions varied through 360 degrees in a relatively small area (Fig 7.2).

British naval reinforcements were the first to arrive off Donegal. Warren had taken seventeen days to reach Donegal with his squadron of four ships. This was slow, given the emergency that had developed. Little could be done about the lack of speed, however, because it was due to the northerly winds that predominated during the last week of September, followed by a mixture of light winds and calms associated with a ridge of high pressure. Had these continued their arrival off Donegal would have been delayed even more. But the situation improved dramatically on 3 October. The wind freshened up and became more southerly. With the wind behind him Warren made much more rapid progress around the coast of Ireland and was approaching Donegal on 10 October.

At this point Warren met up with the frigates based in Loch Swilly, the *Melampus* and *Doris*, which now came under his command. For some time these frigates had been patrolling along the Mayo and Donegal coast and had received no definite news about the break-out of the French from Brest. But they had not seen any sign of them. The apparent non-arrival of the French was good news to Warren, who set about deploying his ships into strategic patrols along the coast. This deployment was delayed by strengthening winds that developed into a full north-west gale later in the day.[3] In such conditions they had to stand further off the coast.

But the French fleet was not far away. Bompard saw the distant outline of the Donegal coast during the evening of this day. He surmised that the frigates that had been pursuing him were probably in his vicinity, although he had been unable to see them for several days. To make sure he would be free of them, Bompard approached Ireland from the northwest in the darkening night with a heading towards Killala Bay. It was Bompard's intention that if he was spotted he would draw any British ships after him as the light faded. With the wind from the north this was easily done and his fleet made rapid progress. At midnight, while still a long way out from land, the French fleet made a dramatic change of direction to northward in order to pass any of the

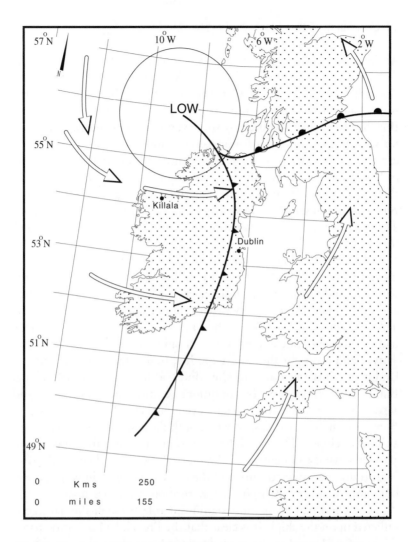

Fig 7.2. Synoptic weather map, 10 October.

British in the dark and reach the north Donegal coast. It was a clever strategy but it involved sailing straight into the wind. The wind was to frustrate it. Although its direction remained constant it strengthened and became a gale. The sea was described as becoming very 'hollow', suggesting a large swell from the Atlantic added to the waves that built up as the wind increased. Northward progress was slow and rough.

11 October: Wind Damage Loads the Dice

At dawn, the three frigates that had shadowed the French all the way from France also arrived on the scene. When the *Amelia, Ethalion* and *Anson* had lost touch on 4 October in poor weather, gales from the south had driven them further to the north than they had intended. But they were then favoured by the reversal of the wind and they met up with Warren on a north-north-west wind. This was timely in the extreme as these frigates added significantly to the firepower available to Warren for the key battle that was about to be fought. He now had three line of battle ships – the *Foudroyant* (80 guns), *Canada* and *Robust* (both 74 guns) – and six frigates – *Magnanime* and *Anson* (both 44 guns), *Amelia* and *Ethalion* (both 38 guns) and *Melampus* and *Doris* (both 36 guns).

Although the low pressure system dominating the weather had moved away over the North Sea by midday, it had deepened and the winds around it became much stronger (Fig 7.3). Gales between north and west had developed everywhere north of a line from Donegal to the Thames estuary in England. At first the French believed their strategy had worked. By midday they were still sailing towards north Donegal. Tory Island was right ahead of them. It appeared that rejecting the easy landing at Killala favoured by the wind had been a risk worth taking. But as the afternoon wore on conditions became much more severe and a swell increased the wave height even further.[4] Then, about noon, Bompard's hopes were dashed when both fleets sighted each other and a chase developed. The British fleet sailed in an east-north-east direction across the wind to intercept the French, who were to their north-west, 'a great distance to windward' and the chase continued 'in very bad and boisterous weather'.[5] By 6pm they were about ten miles apart.

The wind played its most significant role through the damage it inflicted upon the ships. It is clear that the French had not anticipated the severity of weather that now developed, otherwise they would not have put their sails, masts and rigging at risk. The wind became violent – the *Hoche* lost her main topmast. As it fell it shredded the mainsail and brought down the fore and mizen topgallantmasts. This slowed down the entire French fleet. Later, in the evening, there was more bad news. The battering from the high sea caused the *Resolue* to spring a serious leak. A message with this information reached Bompard, but the weather prevented a vital return message that would have initiated a strategy to escape their pursuers (this required the *Resolue* to run onto the coast and signal its distress to draw the British, while the rest sailed

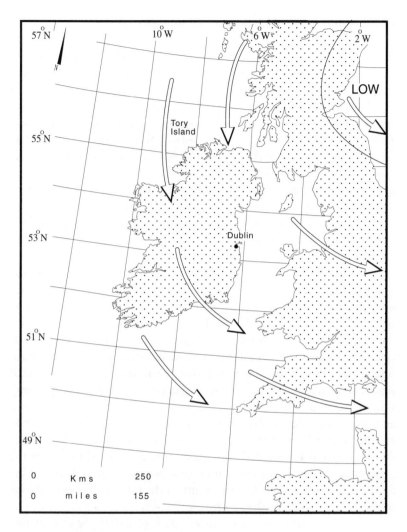

Fig 7.3. Synoptic weather map, 11 October.

to the southwest to land at any suitable point).

The weather also inflicted damage on Warren's ships. In particular, the *Anson* lost some of her masts and sails during the night. This was much less significant than that suffered by the French and did little to hamper the British fleet. But it did keep her from most of the action on the following day because she was not able to keep up with the rest of the squadron.

12 OCTOBER: A SEA BATTLE OFF THE ROSSES

By dawn, the *Hoche* had repaired some of the damage and a new main-sail had been put up; a considerable achievement in the overnight weather. This had eased, although the wind was still northerly (Fig 7.4)

The damaged *Hoche* took up a fairly central position in the battle line formed by the French. Their sequence was *Semillante, Romaine, Bellone, Immortalite, Loire, Hoche, Coquille* and *Embuscade*. The nearest of Warren's fleet was the *Robust* and *Magnanime*, four miles to their rear. The wind meant the only escape was to the southwest where they now headed, still slowed by the damaged *Hoche*. As a result, and with the wind in their favour, it was easy for the British to come up to them at the moment of their own choosing. There is little evidence for the view that Bompart ordered his frigates to retreat while the *Hoche* took on the British alone.

The action began off the Rosses at 7.20am. The *Robust* led the action. Convention was that a ship of the line (74 guns or more) would not fire on a frigate unless the frigate fired first.[6] The *Robust* (74 guns) made for the only French ship of the line, the *Hoche*. It was fired on by the stern chasers of the two French frigates it came up with, which was considered a statement of intent.[7] The *Robust* went around the leeward side of the French line, engaged the *Embuscade* and *Coquille* as it passed and closed with the *Hoche*, whereupon it slowed to keep alongside and maintain its attack. The *Magnanime* was following the *Robust* and fired broadsides on the *Embuscade* and *Coquille*, but had to change course to avoid the *Robust*, passing on its leeward side. The *Loire, Immortalite* and *Bellone* had anticipated this and moved to fire on the *Robust* and *Magnanime* as they tried to avoid each other. This had little effect, and when their fire was returned the French frigates broke off to their escape route in the southwest.

The *Magnanime* swung across the path of the *Hoche* to continue the attack. Warren's other frigates arrived in succession and added to the bombardment. With her rigging shredded, masts tottering, hull riddled, five feet of water in the hold, 25 guns out of action, and numerous crew killed or wounded, the *Hoche* surrendered just before 11am, after three hours 40 minutes (less than the time given in many accounts).[8] The *Embuscade* also surrendered. The others got away, further damaging the *Anson* as they passed.[9] The *Coquille* and *Bellone* were captured later in separate engagements.

The escape of the rest was hindered by a shift in wind direction. It was as if each French move was countered by the wind. During the day

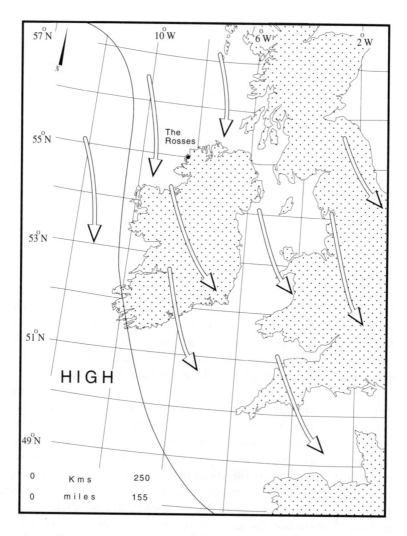

Fig 7.4. Synoptic weather map, 12 October.

the pressure rose from the west and gave a very fine day on land.[10] At sea, it made the winds back to a westerly direction during the battle.[11] In their flight the *Immortalite* and *Resolue*, followed this wind and sailed into Donegal Bay as night fell. Their pursuers were frustrated when within a mile of them the rising pressure caused the wind to drop. The *Loire* and *Semillante* struggled to escape westward during the night with little wind.

13 October: A Lull Before a Storm

The majority of the French fleet were still unbowed. It was important to seize the remaining five frigates because they were 'full of troops and stores, with every necessity for their establishment of their views and plans in Ireland'.[12] Leaving the others with the prizes, the *Canada, Foudroyant* and *Melampus,* went southwards in hot pursuit.

The weather was less boisterous, but it still posed problems for both pursuer and pursued. The ridge of high pressure drifted slowly across Ireland from west to east early in the day, making the winds much lighter and back even further, right round to the south (Fig 7.5). Most of Ireland seemed to benefit from this change. A Letterkenny correspondent to the *Belfast Newsletter* records that this day was almost calm.[13] Off Donegal light winds slowed the chase although at times fresh winds blew from the south. So it was with some difficulty that the *Melampus,* the smallest of the three chasing ships, sailed towards Sligo Bay to look for one or more of the French ships that might attempt to hide there, or even to land troops. This surmise was correct. The *Romaine* had gone there but finding its landing would be strongly opposed, it returned to sea, despite the worsening weather. The *Melampus* took all day to reach and search the bay. It was nearly midnight when it arrived and found the *Resolue* and *Immortalite.*

Another change in the weather now began to take place. As the ridge of high pressure moved away across France a depression pushed eastwards towards Ireland at about latitude 60 N, strengthening the winds. The *Resolue* had closed some of her gun ports, possibly in anticipation of a gale (a common practice in stormy weather). At the moment of her discovery this made her relatively defenceless. During a brief exchange of fire (25 minutes) the *Resolue* was severely damaged and began to take water rapidly. No doubt the damage inflicted in this new attack worsened the leak caused by the storm of 11 October. There was little alternative but to surrender. As soon as the *Resolue* had been boarded the threatening gale broke, which may have been a factor in the *Immortalite* not coming back to her assistance. As it was it was difficult enough for the *Melampus* to remain close to it 'in so violent a storm'. It was so bad that it took six days for the *Melampus* to escort its prize to the Clyde.

The storm that developed during the night nearly brought an end to the *Hoche,* now a prize. After the battle it was taken in tow by the *Robust.* It made little progress because during the day, with very little wind, both ships had some of their battle-damaged masts and rigging

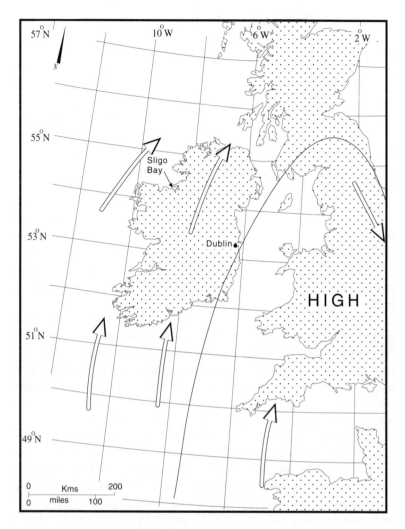

Fig 7.5. Synoptic weather map, 13 October.

collapse. Then the tow-rope broke during the night and the developing storm threatened to sink the *Hoche*. Furious pumping for several days was all that could be done to save it since the *Robust* was too crippled to be of any significant help in the storm that now lashed the coast. Eventually the *Doris* arrived to take the *Hoche* in tow.

15 OCTOBER: A SUCCESSFUL STRATEGY

The *Loire* and the *Semillante* had escaped but their progress had been slow. This was less a product of caution and more a necessity of the weather. The gales that now raged were very severe, 'excessive hard gales' according to the *Canada*'s log, especially on the 14 October, when the log of the *Melampus* records 'lying too under storm stay sails'. It is probable that both French ships also 'lay too', for the worst of the weather. Had their progress been better they would have avoided their next encounter that drew them into a sequence of events ending in the capture of the *Loire*.

On the morning of 15 September, three days since the sea battle off the Rosses, they encountered a coastal patrol sent by Kingsmill from Cork that had taken full advantage of the earlier southerly wind. It consisted of two frigates, the *Revolutionnaire* (38 guns) and the *Mermaid* (32 guns), together with the sloop *Kangaroo* (18 guns). They were near Achill Island when they saw the French to the north and began to chase them.

The pressure had fallen during the night and had increased only slightly in the morning as another depression passed to the northeast (Fig 7.6).[14] Later, the winds veered from south to west as its cold front passed. Behind the cold front, on the southern rim of the depression, the winds were stronger and gales were more widespread compared with the previous day. Storms out in the Atlantic had generated a substantial swell that created added difficulties for the ships.

The wind played a key part in this event, because both pursuer and pursued sailed before the wind, giving the advantage to the larger vessels with their greater amount of sail. Initially the wind was southerly. The *Loire* and *Semillante* edged ahead in the chase as both sets of ships used all the sail they could manage. They headed into the heavy swell and battled against the fresh gales. However, the weather was still good enough to see each other's signals and exchange messages. As a result they separated from each other, a strategy designed to break up the chasing ships.

The two French commanders may have intentionally used the wind in a tactical way during this chase. By running with the wind they not only gained on their pursuers, but also caused the smaller sloop *Kangaroo* to fall behind its companions. Effectively, this reduced the chase to two. Later in the pursuit they separated to ensure that any action would be one against one. This gave a clear advantage in fire-power to the French. Although the *Revolutionnaire* and

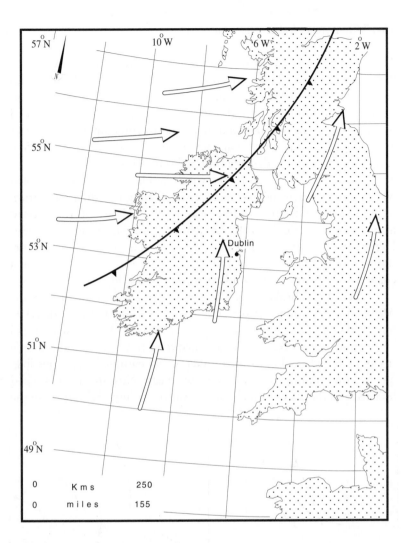

Fig 7.6. Synoptic weather map, 15 October.

Mermaid continued the chase pursuing separate ships, they lost them when the weather deteriorated as the cold front arrived.

Although they had escaped, the French were now even further from their intended escape route back to France. Clearly, they would have to try again, and run the gauntlet of the British fleet still in the area. Their main hope was that the weather would take a hand and cancel out the numerical and other advantages of the fleet in its home waters.

16-17 October: A Titanic Struggle

The stormy weather continued as another depression arrived. When dawn broke the *Mermaid* and *Kangaroo* spotted the *Loire* by itself and set out in pursuit. It was another long chase. The wind was less severe than the previous day and in the afternoon the *Kangaroo*, emboldened by the presence of the *Mermaid*, managed to come up with the *Loire* and engage her. It had only half the firepower of the *Loire* and having sustained considerable damage dropped out of the pursuit.

The *Loire* was trapped by the wind. While the wind was between west and south each successive chase was driving it further away from its home, into colder and stormier seas to the northeast, of which it had little experience (Fig 7.7a). Its homeward route was to the southwest. Depressions tracking in a northeasterly direction gave few such opportunities. If only they would follow a west – east track there was a chance of more northerly winds as it passed by (Fig 7.7b).

When dawn broke on 17 September the *Loire* realised that the *Mermaid* was the only pursuer. The *Loire* was a 40 gun frigate of 1,100 tons, while the *Mermaid* was a 32-gun frigate of 693 tons. Neither had been seriously damaged, so the *Loire* had the advantage. In addition, the troops on board would provide musket fire if boarding became possible. due to a ridge of high pressure to the southeast. Now that the wind had lessened and the sea was much calmer, the possibility of closing with the

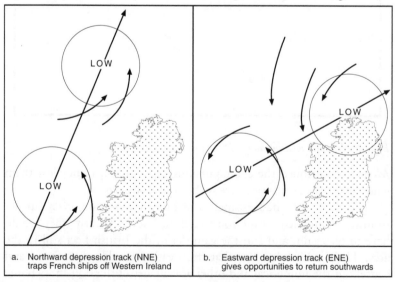

a. Northward depression track (NNE) traps French ships off Western Ireland

b. Eastward depression track (ENE) gives opportunities to return southwards

Fig 7.7. Depression tracks and the winds off the west coast.

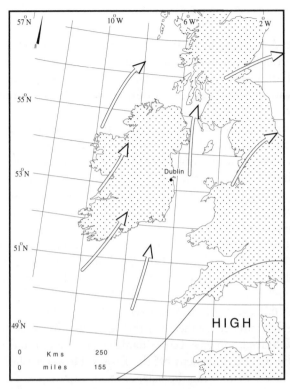

Fig 7.8. Synoptic weather map, 17 October.

Mermaid and boarding her was strong. The *Loire* shortened its sail to slow down and then engaged. It was a little before 7am. The *Loire* tried to use the advantage of the good sea conditions to draw close and board. But skilful manoeuvring by Lieutenant Halliday made this impossible. A sudden backing of the wind to the south-south-west was sufficient for the *Mermaid* to manoeuvre for a damaging broadside with little response (Fig 7.8). Such skilful positioning was typical of the encounter, as the *Mermaid* closed within a pistol shot and then moved away with agility and precision not matched by the *Loire*. But the *Loire* had its own heavy guns and made them tell, matching the accuracy of the *Mermaid*'s own fire. Both vessels sustained heavy damage to their sails, masts and rigging. The *Mermaid*'s hull was also damaged and began to take in water. Although it was crippled, the *Loire* was reluctant to approach the *Mermaid*'s guns and was itself too shot up to continue. It put before the wind and soon disappeared. The *Mermaid* had won a remarkable victory.

The trials of the *Mermaid* were not over. Its crew was tested to the full by the gales and heavy rain that descended on it in the afternoon. The strong wind blew away the remains of the mainsail, and in raising a replacement foresail, the foremasts and yards collapsed onto the deck and the ship found itself at the mercy of a violent sea.[15] After that, it took two days to struggle to Lough Swilly.

18 October: The End of the Chase

Few on board the *Loire* thought their troubles were over. As well as being far from a friendly anchorage they had also sustained serious damage. The swell on the sea now affected all the seas around Ireland from the Old Head of Kinsale in the south to Malin Head in the north, and beyond.

But the weather began to offer some hope. As the depression to the north moved on the winds veered to the northwest – at last (Fig.7.9). This was the first time since the engagement between the two fleets began that the winds were favourable for a return journey to France. But the *Loire* was unable to seize this opportunity. Not only were significant repairs needed for the homeward journey, but it found it had not shaken off the pursuit.

When dawn broke the *Loire* found itself in the company of two more of Warren's fleet. To the windward appeared the *Anson*, a 44 gun frigate, comparable in many ways to the 40-gun *Loire*. However, the relevant comparison between the vessels was the damage each had sustained so far. The damage to the *Anson* over the past few days was about the same as that suffered by the *Loire* the day before in its battle with the *Mermaid*. Indeed, some of *Anson*'s damage had been from the *Loire* itself after the main engagement off the Rosses. However, there was an additional factor that swung the balance against the *Loire*. The sloop *Kangaroo* was with the *Anson*. Although it had been damaged by the *Loire* two days before, its crew had managed to carry out considerable repairs in the meantime. This made the *Kangaroo* a significant force given the damaged state of the two frigates. The *Anson* and the *Kangaroo* had met up during the night and stayed together because of the *Anson*'s poor condition.

It was about 8.30am when the *Loire* was spotted and another chase began. At first it was not obvious to the *Anson* and *Kangaroo* which ship they were pursuing. It was a measure of the amount of damage sustained by the *Loire* on the previous day that its appearance had changed so much as to make recognition difficult for those who, after engaging it in battle, would expect to know it. They had to get close to be sure of its identity.

The wind was now from the northwest. The Loire was leeward of its pursuers and struggled to make headway in a southerly direction. The *Kangaroo* was some distance to the windward of the *Anson* and normally would have been left behind in the chase, as happened a few days earlier. But it was the least disabled of the three and with a

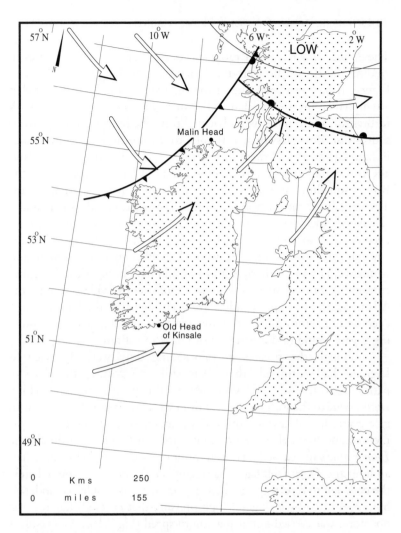

Fig 7.9. Synoptic weather map, 18 October.

following wind it managed to keep up. It took two hours for the *Anson* to catch the *Loire*. There was only a little fight left in the French frigate. Between 10.30am and 11.45am the *Anson* and *Loire* slugged it out with broadsides until the *Kangaroo* arrived. Although the *Kangaroo* was initially on the receiving end of the *Loire's* guns its own broadsides brought down more of the French ship's masts and rigging. Having six feet of water in the hold and now being virtually defenceless, the *Loire* surrendered.

20 OCTOBER: AN UNWELCOME HOMECOMING

The *Immortalite* had been more successful than the other frigates in eluding the British fleet around Ireland and making its way back to France. It had also been one of the survivors of the French fleet that attempted an invasion at Bantry Bay in 1796. Now it was sailing back to Brest on a favourable wind backing from the northwest to the west-south-west. Being less than 100 miles to the northwest of Brest, it was in familiar waters and there was every prospect of a friendly, dry, land ahead. Despite this, it was keeping a careful lookout because of the British squadron normally on the approaches to the Brittany coast. The captain of the *Immortalite*, Jean-Francois Legrand, was taking a calculated risk. In most circumstances a less direct route would have been advised, to avoid the blockade, even to the extent of heading for a port further to the south. But with a high likelihood of persistent and strong westerly to southerly winds it would have been a slow and time-consuming process to follow a route sufficiently wide out into the Atlantic. Instead, hopes would have been high that the blockade had been withdrawn to pursue the invasion fleet and that a single returning frigate would find it easier to slip back into Brest.

Although the frigates on blockading duty were dispersed as Legrand had surmised, there was still one frigate, the *Fisgard*, patrolling to the west of Ushant. At 8am it spotted the approaching *Immortalite* to the west at no great distance, and it turned towards it to give chase. Just after noon the *Fisgard* came level and the action commenced. Both vessels were of similar size and firepower. Initially the *Immortalite*'s fire caused a large amount of damage and after only half an hour the *Fisgard* fell back, its rigging 'cut to pieces'.[16] Immediately the crew fell to repairing the damage and, with only light to moderate breezes ensured by a ridge of high pressure that covered the area, the operation was carried out at maximum speed (Fig 7.10). As a result it was very soon ready to get after its prey. It took barely an hour to catch up with the French frigate again and re-engage her. There is no doubt that in other weather conditions this would not have been possible. The mutual exchange of cannon fire did immense damage to both vessels, including damage below the water line, and when the *Immortalite*'s captain and first lieutenant were killed, it surrendered.

Despite the damage to both vessels, the *Fisgard* was able to escort its prize to Plymouth, aided by moderate weather and south to south-westerly winds from the high pressure to the south. This prize was largely a result of the superior seamanship of the *Fisgard*'s crew, no

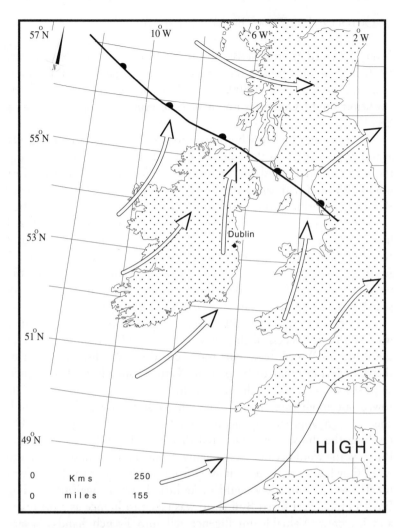

Fig 7.10. Synoptic weather map, 20 October.

doubt energised at the prospect of receiving a share in the value of their prize. The engagement was a rare occasion when comparable frigates were matched and the outcome largely depended on the skill of the crews alone. To many it confirmed the value of experience gained from long periods at sea on blockade duty and coastal patrol rather than being blockaded in a port.

27 OCTOBER: THE THIRD FRENCH FLEET

Savary returned to Killala Bay from Rochefort with reinforcements. With an additional frigate, the *Venus*, it had been possible to ship even more troops (this time 1,800, under General Cortez). They had left Rochefort on 12 October without news of Humbert nor of Bompart's fleet.[17]

It was a considerable achievement to have completed the voyage yet again without meeting the enemy, who were now fully alert, scouring the seas around Ireland for French ships. Savary had left Rochefort unobserved and had sailed the longer westward route to avoid them. But this had included one false start. After being at sea for six days they were driven back by strong winds and rough seas. Conditions on board had been so severe that some of the sick had to be returned to land and two ships (the *Renard* and *Ferrailleur*) dropped out of the expedition. [18] At the second attempt the journey was more comfortable and the weather no longer threatened their voyage. Once in Irish waters, Savary sailed straight to Killala as he was now familiar with the coastline.

As before, they arrived off Killala flying British colours. The ruse was even more successful this time. Captain Bull, the duty officer of the Prince of Wales Regiment, was ordered to take dispatches out to them, believing them to be part of Warren's squadron. The French ships stood well clear of the shallow inshore water, so Bull had to be rowed out about three miles, although the southerly (offshore) wind, ahead of an approaching depression, helped them (Fig 7.11). On reaching the ships, they discovered their mistake and tried to escape. But now the wind became their enemy. It was a only a moderate breeze when they had started out, but away from the shelter of the land it was much stronger, and they could make little headway against it.[19] The French quickly captured Bull (who was taken to France as a prisoner) and his crew. Valuable intelligence fell into French hands. Savary learned that Humbert had been defeated and Bompart's squadron had been captured and scattered. Had this information not been forth-coming, it had been Savary's intention to land the troops and go straight back to France for more. As Bull was interrogated, the cutter *Fox* from Warren's squadron appeared and fired warning shots at them, probably to alert the rest of the squadron cruising in the area. There was no reason for Savary to linger any further and, anxious to avoid the British, set off back to France about 7pm.

Meanwhile, the identity of the ships had become clear to those watching on the shore. The word spread like wildfire. Stock recorded

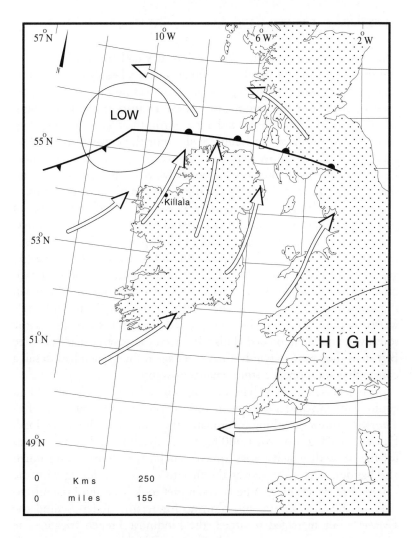

Fig 7.11. Synoptic weather map, 27 October.

some of the panic that ensued. People fled without waiting to see whether the French would land. A vigorous cold front in the rear of the depression arrived and made the weather cold and stormy (Fig 7.11). The road was soon deep in mud and most had to walk. The wind was 'furious' and the refugees were buffeted by strong gusts of wind and assailed by heavy showers of hail and thundery rain. [20]

28 October: The Wind Dictates a Chase

This was a day of two parts. The previous day had ended with storms. But this one opened with relatively quiet weather, largely influenced by high pressure to the south (Fig 7.12). There was no hint of a deep low pressure about to move into the northwest. Instead, the wind was light and the weather quite pleasant. To the north, the *Doris* was still struggling to tow the *Hoche* to Lough Swilly. For the crews of both damaged ships the improvement in the weather was very welcome. Elsewhere, in the shelter of the north Mayo coast, the slack wind slowed French progress, but it also slowed Warren's pursuing ships.

In the early afternoon, as they passed north of the Staggs of Broadhaven, Savary's frigates were spotted for the first time by a new squadron of British ships. There were two ships of the line, the *Caesar* (80 guns) and the *Terrible* (74 guns) and a frigate, the *Melpomene* (38 guns). The wind was so light that they could do little but look at each other, although an occasional breeze allowed a slow pursuit. But when the low pressure system from the North Atlantic began to push eastwards in the afternoon, the wind veered from the southeast to the southwest and strengthened. This reinforced the advantage of the three British as they were to windward. So yet again the French had to sail a course that was opposite from what they wanted.

They closed quickly. The French were laden with armament and equipment and had no hope of out-distancing their pursuers. The *Concorde* threw anything overboard that would lighten its load. During the chase arms for 1,500 men went overboard, sixteen cannons (of the 38 with which it was armed), anchors, watercasks and much else besides. The *Terrible* was the first to catch up, closing with the *Concorde* in the evening. A fierce encounter took place until the mizenmast of the *Terrible* was hit. Slowing for repairs, it fell behind the *Concorde* but managed to attack the hindmost French frigate. The night brought some respite for the French. But Savary was too experienced to dismiss the threat of the *Terrible*. He expected the repairs to have been completed by the morning and the action renewed.

Without firing another shot the French were to benefit significantly from another event as well. The wind had been increasing throughout the evening and now became very strong. The low pressure had moved much closer and was beginning to affect the weather throughout Ireland. As the pressure fell the pressure gradient steepened sharply, significantly increasing the wind speeds.[21] At 11pm that night, the wind became so strong that the largest ship of the chasing group,

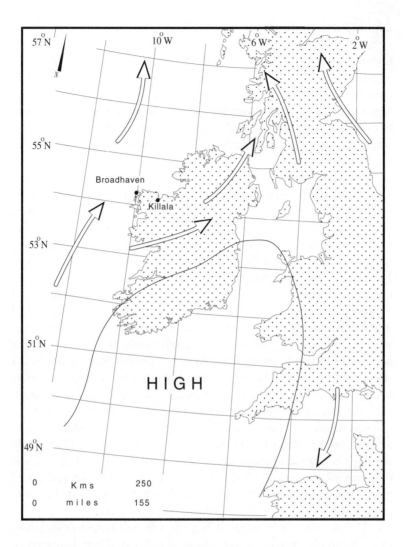

Fig 7.12. Synoptic weather map, 28 October.

the *Caesar*, had two of its masts damaged, and as they fell they demol-
ished one of the sails – a constant risk when a mast breaks and falls. At
that point the *Caesar* had been leading the chase, but now it fell behind
the other two vessels and was lost sight of in the early hours of the following morning.

29-30 October: Rescued by the Wind

Overnight and into the morning the pressure continued to fall, reaching very low levels and remained low for several days.[22] But over a wide area the winds were quite moderate. The few gales recorded in ship logs appear to have been localised. The damage to the *Caesar* was due to one of these. The wind had removed the largest British man of war from the chase and significantly improved the chances for the escape of the French.

From daylight the French made rapid headway to the northwest and kept ahead of the two chasing ships until about noon. The smallest French frigate, the *Venus*, began to slow and since the French were staying together, the gap narrowed quickly. At this point Savary had to make a difficult choice between support for the *Venus* and maximising the chances for the escape of his other ships. Since there were four French and only two British ships he decided they should scatter. So the *Concorde* headed to the west, across the face of the south-west wind. The *Melpomene* followed in pursuit. The *Terrible*, which had now carried out repairs, tried to follow the *Medee* and *Franchise* to the west-north-west. The *Venus* sailed directly before the wind (from the southwest), but was mostly ignored as the pursuit was for the bigger ships. The size of the *Terrible* told and by 4pm it was only two miles behind the two frigates it was chasing. As the light failed the pursuit took the British frigates on divergent courses until they lost contact.

Overnight the chase changed its shape. The only two ships in chase at dawn on 30 October were the *Terrible* and the *Medee*. Throughout the day the chase continued to the northwest. The French frigate was only two miles ahead and had little hope of escape. The *Terrible* passed gun-carriages and horses being jettisoned to lighten its load. But once more it was the weather that eventually came to its rescue.

The pursuit continued until 5pm. Squalls and rain were spreading from the south ahead of a warm front (Fig 7.13). These had reached the north Mayo coast by midday, being recorded in a number of ships' logs off both Broadhaven and Killala Bay. Without warning an unexpected squall of wind engulfed the *Terrible* and brought down a number of its sails and damaged the masts. The suddenness and violence of the event for a moment brought chaos and confusion to the deck. It marked the end of the chase. The *Terrible* had to stop to deal with the damage and the French frigate sailed out of sight and on to its unexpected freedom.

Savary's strategy had worked. All four French frigates escaped. The

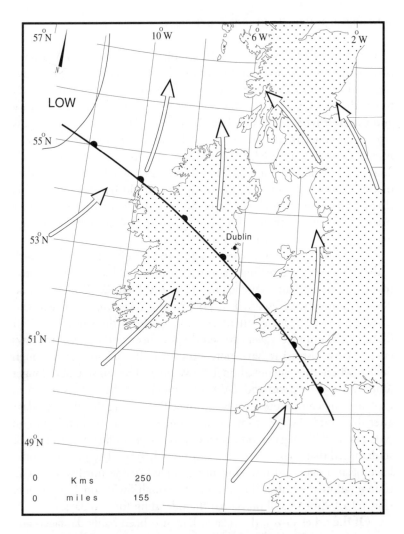

Fig 7.13. Synoptic weather map, 30 October.

odds had been heavily against this, but the weather had played a major role in cancelling out the physical advantages of the *Ceasar* and *Terrible*. Both had been badly damaged by strong winds at the moment when they had the upper hand and were poised to take their prize. As a result their prey escaped. All four French frigates met up during their return voyage and re-entered Rochefort together on 4 November.[23]

1 NOVEMBER: PRISONERS AND PRIZES

In the series of actions from 12-18 October the ships under Warren's command captured seven of the original French fleet, three others having made good their escape to France. But there was still much to do to get them safely to port. This was not merely to confirm the victory and to arrest rebel leaders on board, but to get the prize money. This would be equal to the value of the boats, their contents and head money for those captured, all of which would add up to a considerable amount.[24] Although Warren as the commander would get a great deal of this, individual ships making a capture would have a considerable share divided between all the crew. So they worked hard to save their prizes. Warren left them with his frigates and went ahead to Lough Swilly to send news of the victory to Kingsmill.[25]

The main prize was the *Hoche*, with Wolfe Tone on board. Although it was one of four captured in the initial action, it had too much storm and battle damage to follow the *Coquille, Embuscade* and *Bellone* as they were escorted to port by the *Magnanime, Amelia* and *Ethalion*. After a huge effort to save the *Hoche* in the storm of 13/14 October the crippled *Robust* passed the tow over to the *Doris* two days later. Many historians have noted the time it took to reach Lough Swilly, where they anchored on 1 November. The considerably longer journeys of the *Resolue* and *Loire* took much less time. This has been explained by continuous stormy weather. But during the nineteen days after the battle, the log of the *Doris* recorded 'strong' or 'hard' gales on only two and 'fresh gales' on a further three days. In fact, the *Hoche* was so damaged that its progress was exceptionally slow. The journey would have been longer had the wind not changed to the northwest just in time to allow them into the entrance to Lough Swilly on 1 November (Fig 7.14). Storms still prevented them landing for two days.

Of the other prizes, the *Resolue* had also been badly damaged and was taking a lot of water when captured by the *Melampus* on 14 October. It was towed in persistent strong south and south-west winds. With little choice but to sail before the wind, and unable to turn into Lough Swilly, they went on to Greenock on the River Clyde, arriving on 19 October.[26] The battered *Loire* had been taken on 18 October and was towed by the *Kangaroo*, attended by the *Anson*. On that day the winds had veered to the northwest behind a cold front, so the prize was taken southwards to Plymouth. This north wind was the saviour of three Irish officers on board the *Loire* – Corbett, Hamilton and MacGuire. In Plymouth they were unrecognised and were sent to

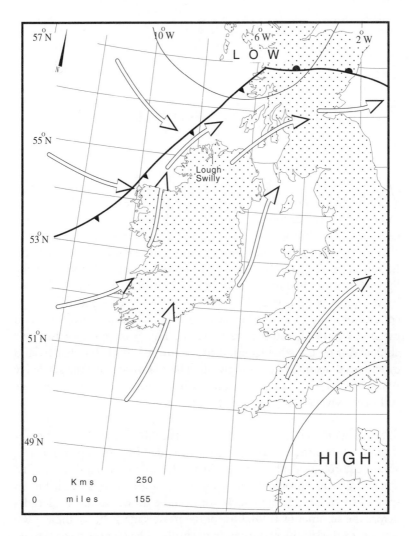

Fig 7.14. Synoptic weather map, 31 October.

France in a prisoner exchange. [27]

For Cornwallis in Dublin, the greatest prize was on board the *Hoche*. Wolfe Tone was recognised among the French officers when they landed. He was imprisoned and eventually paid the ultimate price for being a founder member of the United Irishmen and one of the chief protagonists behind French attempts to invade Ireland since 1796.

8

THE WEATHER AND REBELLION

At the end of the eighteenth century the weather of Europe was emerging from a period when conditions were quite different from those we experience today. This period is known as the Little Ice Age. Over much of Europe it had reached its nadir a century earlier. Its characteristic winters were distinguished by their severity and length. Its summers tended to be short, cool and often wet and stormy, as the Spanish Armada had found to its cost when wrecked on the Irish coast by the summer storms of 1588.[1] As the climate emerged from these conditions European weather acquired much greater variability and extreme weather became more frequent. This was typical of Britain's climate during the seventeenth century and it is probable that Ireland experienced a similar climatic swing. The recovery from the Little Ice Age was slow and haphazard, and Irish records show that there were still many severe winters and poor summers. [2]

SUMMER WEATHER IN EIGHTEENTH-CENTURY IRELAND: A partial snapshot of eighteenth century weather is provided by a survey of 'remarkable meteorological phenomena' in the Census of Ireland for 1851.[3] There are many problems in using information of this kind, but in spite of these some broad conclusions can be drawn about the decades before the summer of 1798. One of the most remarkable of these is the wetness of the summers during that century. The Census record shows that up to 50 per cent more remarkably wet summers were recorded in the second half of the century than in the first half. Throughout the entire period extremes of wetness were much more frequent than extremes of dryness or heat. Indeed, the Census record only mentions extreme heat about once every ten years (1750, 1760, 1765, 1778, 1785, 1794). This record does not identify the summer of 1798 as being in any way worthy of note, either with regard to its heat and dryness on the one hand or its rain, wind and storminess on the other.

In addition to this rather general picture more detailed year-to-year information about the summer weather in Ireland is contained in the meteorological records compiled by Rutty in Dublin.[4] Taking all the summers into account he concluded that wet summers were 25 per cent more frequent than dry, hot summers. This was much more strongly a feature of the period after 1750.

From 1792 a variety of detailed climatic statistics are available from the analysis of systematic instrumental observations, particularly those made by Kirwan in Dublin. These shed a great deal of light upon the weather during the years leading up to the rising in 1798. The years 1792 to 1797 were very wet years.[5] But the wetness did not have a great deal to do with particularly high rainfall totals. These were generally less than 750mm (30 inches) a year. Rather, the key to the climate's wetness lay in the high number of days on which rain occurred. Only one year had less than nine months when the rain did not fall on more than half the days. Indeed most months had many more wet days than that. Each of the months May to September, so critical for the 1798 rising, were among these wet months.[6] Such summers must have been very dreary and unhealthy, especially for the poor and the peasantry. For five of the six years before 1798, 21 of a possible total of 25 summer months had rain on more than half of their days. All this adds up to a wetness spread throughout the summer months, albeit in broken spells that normally maintained a constant level of moisture in the soil for crops and favoured the prospect of good harvests.

Much of this was noted by a remarkable character who wandered through Ireland the year before the rising. The Frenchman, Francois de Lactocnaye, set out from Dublin on 25 May 1796 and re-entered the same city a year later.[7] He soon came to the conclusion 'the rain in this country is terrible; it seems to penetrate to the bones, and would make you shiver with cold in the middle of summer', and noted that 'I was wet to the skin nearly every day'.[8] It was the most frequent feature of the climate upon which he commented, but he found a novel-looking solution in the form of an umbrella attachment to his swordstick that was the source of much mirth as he passed by.[9]

But the summer of 1798 was different. The succession of wet summers came to a sudden halt. The contrast was quite extreme. In Kirwan's record the entire year had only one single month with more than 50 per cent of the days with some rainfall. This summer dryness, that so benefited the rising of May-June, was a product of successive ridges of high pressure spreading their influence over Ireland, mostly from the south. In earlier wet years these high pressure extensions had not reached so far north. Their invasion into more northerly latitudes during the 1798 summer, particularly in its early months, was far from typical. The result was to divert or block the advance of depressions from the west. Even so, Ireland was on the margins of this effect. When the shadow of these depressions fell over the north of Ireland the weather would contrast strongly across the country.

It has been claimed that the summer of the previous year, 1797, provided the best opportunity for the United Irishmen to rise and for the French to invade Ireland. But as far as the weather was concerned this would have been a particularly poor summer in which to make such a bid. For the two months of May and June Kirwan registered 40 days of rain in both 1796 and 1797, in contrast to a mere seventeen in 1798. Even in Ulster there were 50 per cent more days of rain for the same period in 1797 compared with 1798. For some areas the summer of 1797 was not just wet, it was exceptional. The Kilmaine diary notes it as the wettest ever remembered. Notwithstanding the favourable political circumstances of 1797, the impact of rain upon the rebels in Wexford, Wicklow and elsewhere in 1798 makes it difficult to see how the rebellion could have flourished had it been conducted in the summer weather of 1797. However, the evidence also suggests that this factor would not have been built into any strategic planning and there would have been a very wet, unpleasant campaign.

During the summer of 1798 one month stands out as being quite different from the rest – the month of July. By any standards it was an extremely rainy month. Set in an otherwise notably dry summer, its wetness is even more pronounced. First of all, it was the wettest month of the year. At Edgeworthstown there was an amazing 161.8mm (6.37 ins) of rain and out of 23 rain days in Dublin it rained nearly every day, often heavily. Only the month of January came remotely close to these totals. Again, this was not a localised feature. It was common across both Ireland and Britain to a latitude about as far north as Belfast.[10] While it made life miserable for everyone involved in the conflict, it was a much greater help to those who were isolated, on the defensive and taking refuge in remote areas, rather than those on the offensive. The Wicklow mountains, normally regarded as a wilderness, seemed even more impenetrable as a result. The Killoughram Forest was a similar refuge for many in north-west Wexford. But neither of them were long-term options for the rebels. The rain would stop eventually and few would savour a long-term stay. However, as long as they provided protection while waiting for the arrival of the French, they were bearable. A second measure of July's wetness is that its rainfall total was not surpassed until July 1822. Although this is based on the continuous Dublin record, it is also a feature of the rainfall record of England and Wales.[11] So, in terms of the long-term climatic record, the rainfall of July 1798 was fairly extreme. The reason for this lies in the wider atmospheric circulation. The normal summer anticyclonic influences from the south simply seem to have disappeared. They were elsewhere, in much lower latitudes than usual.[12]

However, a word of caution is necessary in attributing too great a significance to July's wetness. It was probably a feature of the eighteenth-century climate in Ireland that the month of July was relatively wet. To the insurgents and the military, the arrival of the rain at the end of June and in early July would have come as no surprise. Its arrival would have been regarded as only a matter of time. It was typical for July to be the wettest month of the summer as well as one of the wettest of the year. Edward Wakefield in his survey of Ireland in 1812, ranked July as the second rainiest month of the year after December.[13] It was just a little unusual for it to be the wettest month and for the rainfall total to be so high.

One of the benefits of dry weather in summer is that it is often much warmer, at least during the daytime. During the dry days of the 1798 summer there were few occasions when either the wind or cloud spoilt this. Being wrapped in a blanket of warmth does make destitution and hunger marginally more bearable, provided it is not to excess. However, the temperature contrasts between the moist summer days of 1797 and the dry days of 1798 would have reinforced the severity of the heat, just as some commentators noted. May, June, August and September displaced their temperature ranges upwards between 2 and 5°C.[14] Since July was normally wet in any case its temperatures were not very different from previous years. However, in terms of comfort and health, the impact of the warmth and dryness was considerable. A Quaker diarist noted that 'a long period of fine weather was granted as well as uncommon health, for we rarely heard of any sickness, and previously Ballitore seldom passed through a summer without being visited by fever amongst the poor'.[15] Even the military experienced these benefits, much to the satisfaction of the director general of military hospitals who euphemistically noted that the good weather was 'no disadvantage to their general health'.[16]

EXPECTATIONS OF THE WEATHER: As we begin to re-discover and understand some of the principal features of the late eighteenth-century climate in Ireland, it is possible to identify the weather expectations of the protagonists, whether they used that information to their advantage and if so, whether the outcomes were significantly affected.

1. Weather and the insurgents. If the peasants who feared being burnt out of their homes and tortured by the yeomen had been praying for a miracle, it must have seemed like one when the weather dried up and became so fine that they could escape the terror by sleeping and living outdoors. With little expectation of such weather and with a desperate population undoubtedly praying for deliverance, the transformation of the weather could hardly be seen as anything other than a miracle. It was a small step from seeing it as a means of escape from immediate persecution to an expectation of complete deliverance from the rule of those they had been taught were heretics.

The idea of providence had been strong in all Christian traditions for many centuries. It had a powerful influence on how Catholics and Protestants as well as Dissenters such as Presbyterians and Quakers reacted to events, particularly natural events. Weather was one way by which God was seen to work through the natural order, since it was completely beyond any human influence. In County Wexford, the timely arrival of the dry weather and the opportunistic (though undoubtedly sincere) interpretation by the clergy gave an added authority to the priests. A number of them took key leadership roles from then onwards and had a significant input into the rebel strategy. Some of these behaved as though they were invincible, as if (turning a familiar phrase on its head) 'right is might'. This sense of invincibility may also have been based on a certain numerical logic since the rebels vastly outnumbered their opponents. It is conveyed in several of the key engagements, for example at Bunclody, Arklow and New Ross, and seems to have led to a disdain of carefully considered strategy.[17] The battle of Arklow illustrates it particularly well. The rebels arrived late in the day after delays that allowed a significant reinforcement to reach the garrison. The priests placed greater importance on providing indulgences and charms and saying masses than to take any strategic initiative. An earlier arrival would also have favoured a different out-come for the smoke screen at the Fishery. Instead, it was a loyalists who saw a providence at work, noting 'but the Almighty caused the wind to shift, so that they were confounded by their own devices', and, 'an error of conduct which, providentially ... caused the ruin of their scheme'.[18]

In the midland counties the rebellion was effectively over after the first few days. There was a different kind of leadership and a much weaker sense of providence, although Teeling's view was undoubtedly widespread that 'the virtuous have the special protection of heaven' and could speak of 'an all-ruling providence'.[19] However, the organisation and strategy of the United Irishmen in the midland counties had been fatally disrupted by the arrests of the leadership just before the planned outbreak. Few priests filled the gap and the leadership of Alymer and others was much more sensitive to the strategic realities of their position and the realistic possibility of success. They had no great story of miraculous deliverance to encourage them. There was no equivalent to Oulart, Enniscorthy and Wexford. And things got no better when Wexford columns joined them. The weather gave no 'sign'. In fact the dryness tended to make them somewhat more vulnerable in their bogland refuges.

The Protestant Dissenters in Ulster were much more cerebral in their theology than their Wexford counterparts. Millenial ideology had both pro- and anti-revolutionary expressions, particularly in the Presbyterian community.[20] It was the 'sign of the times' (the French Revolution) that indicated that God's Providence was at work hastening the 'end times' that strengthened the resolve of many United Irishmen in Ulster. As United Irishmen, they had prepared a strategy for capturing both Antrim and Down. This went ahead. But there is less evidence that providential significance was attached to the weather compared with Wexford. At Ballynahinch, Munroe's refusal to attack at night appears to have been due less to his certainty that providence would deliver a daytime victory than his own romantic predisposition that would not take an ungenerous advantage of the enemy.[21]

But eventually the good weather ended. No clue is given as to what providential interpretation of this was given. In fact it may not have been necessary. Other motives had probably grown by this time, if they had not existed before. The rebels did not simply put down their arms and return home as soon as the weather broke, nor did their priests repent and call others to do the same. Reality is always more complex. For many the basic reasons for rebellion had not been removed and they were still deeply attached to their cause. The expectation of the French and the instinct for survival all energised the final days. The break in the weather and the final collapse in Wexford did not coincide. There was still much hard fighting. Even then thousands left the county to continue the struggle elsewhere.

The weather, especially the wind, worked out its influence upon events without it being harnessed strategically. There were moments of tactical awareness that stand out. In towns, wind-driven smoke from roofs set on fire by rebels proved to be a tactical problem for defenders, as at Enniscorthy (although whether this was a genuine tactical ploy is difficult to establish) and Arklow (where the tactic was probably deliberate). In the neighbouring county of Carlow the Wexfordmen achieved some military success by opportunistically taking advantage of the weather conditions they found. But equally on their return, after finding little support there, they were unprepared for, and fell foul of, the weather in the Scullogue Gap. In the debate about taking the struggle from the Wicklow Mountains onto the plains of Meath and Kildare towards Ulster the relative advantages of the geographies of the mountains and plains were an important consideration. But the mountains were already wet and they were even more inhospitable with the exceptionally wet July. The Wexford leaders were anxious for a more friendly environment and forcefully carried the argument. For most of them the Wicklow weather was quite alien to their experience.

In fact, it was a common experience throughout both the early and late summer risings for those who marched beyond their own counties and familiar environment to become increasingly ill at ease in their unfamiliar surroundings. Wexfordmen soon returned from Carlow while Carlowmen abandoned them in the mists at the Wexford border. Wexfordmen heading into south Wicklow turned back while many others who left the mountains for Meath deserted and headed for home. Even those who stayed in Wicklow soon 'excused themselves by reason of the inclemency of the weather'.[22] Desertions also plagued Humbert in his advance from Mayo, increasing as he left the mountains behind and marched through the bogs. New, unfamiliar environments were a struggle and alien to the recruits.

Some Irish leaders argued strongly that they should stay and fight on familiar ground. Holt argued vigorously to sustain the rebel activity in the mountains of Wicklow rather than taking the struggle onto the plains. Fighting on their own territory was much more successful for the rebels. The military became exasperated by the regular experience of having their prey disappear into the mists and clouds that frequently shrouded the summits, whenever the summits could be seen through the drenching rain. This was part of the rebel ability to use the total environment as a refuge. Moore only came near to successfully campaigning against them when he had special highland troops relatively familiar with the remote, wet mountain landscape (they were described as being 'temperamentally and physically suited to the task'), when he chose the weather and when he adopted an appropriate strategy.[23]

The French were as unfamiliar with the west of Ireland weather as with its drumlin and boggy terrain. Landing in weather similar to the French summer may have shaped French expectations. As a result, it is possible that weather factors were discounted in favour of the necessity of waiting for reinforcements, since the quality of recruits that flocked to their standard did not meet up to their requirements. But the fine spell of weather was insufficient to improve the marching conditions along their route. Whether bogs or drumlins, the terrain was a wet, formidable obstacle for marching several thousand men. Even the Irish leaders with Humbert were not from the west and may have been unaware how little the good weather they had encountered early in the campaign would have dried out the country ahead of them.

2. Weather and the military: While Irish leaders showed little anxiety about the weather and only a limited ability to use it strategically, this was not always the case with the military forces ranged against them. There is some evidence for the strategic use of the weather conditions from early on in the conflict. The battle of Newtownmountkennedy was the first occasion that weather conditions were strategically deployed, when Lt. Bourganey successfully used a smoke screen. The awareness of how fire and smoke could combine in town warefare led the Wexford garrison to strip the roofs of houses near the town gate to prevent a recurrence of the Enniscorthy experience. Another occasion was Asgill's successful use of the fog at Scullabogue Gap. But these were mostly responses to immediate weather conditions. There was little anticipation of weather developments in the short term. The closest to this was when Moore was prepared to wait for the weather to improve in Wicklow before continuing his campaign there, but that may have been as much a matter of necessity and the wellbeing of his troops as for any other strategic consideration.

While Moore was prepared to wait for the rain to stop there does not appear to have been similar consideration for waiting for a break in the fine weather. It was inevitable that the spell of fine, dry weather of May-June would end eventually. But it still came as a surprise. When it did arrive it was at an inconvenient moment for Moore. The severe early morning rain of 19 June delayed his planned attack on Lacken Hill. Clearly, none of the generals had been sensitive to the advancing cloud, increasing humidity and changing wind the previous evening. Their strategy appears to have been subject only to the weather of the moment. If ever there was an occasion to demonstrate an awareness of the weather and its strategic usefulness it could have been at the end of this long, rainless period. But there was no apparent anticipation of the change.

Even so, Moore was probably an exception to other commanders in his awareness and assessment of the environment in which he campaigned. In unfamiliar terrain he was careful to conduct reconnaissance in a regular detailed manner, and his brother recorded that after a tiring march, when others rested 'he galloped all round the country, examined every wood and eminence, questioned the country people respecting every road and path, and compared their different accounts with a good map'.[24] But such awareness did not appear to extend to the weather, which not only caught him out at New Ross but again during his first incursion into Glenmalure. There, his decision not to take tents was partly due to ignorance of how wet the mountains could be. It led to great suffering and did nothing to dispel the view that the area was a wilderness in which its summer cold, wind and rain were as formidable as obstacles to human mobility and survival as its steep slopes, narrow valleys, high summits and boggy ground.

His experience of moving his troops on Irish roads was also quite salutory. As much as he was struck by the wetness of the mountains, he also found the dustiness of Irish roads quite remarkable. It must be said that the roads in much of the country were regarded as good and were often kept in excellent repair. They were well made and were used by few heavy wagons. They were not normally bordered by hedgerows and trees, so they dried quickly after rain. However, dry weather conditions gave rise to excessive dust clouds visible from miles away. This receives frequent comment in accounts of the Wexford rising. The dust made troops and cavalry and other large groups on the move very conspicuous, while they had limited vision themselves. Heat and dust on the march were an exhausting combination, and when advancing from Cork to Waterford, Moore found that 'the heat and dust are intolerable'.[25] William Farrell of Carlow described the conditions more vividly: '... such heaps of dust on the road as I never saw before from the long continued heat and drought. The horses and chaise raised it in such clouds that we were obliged to keep the glasses up and when we went on a little father we heard the noise of horsemen approaching us. They soon came up and when both parties met the dust rose so thick a cloud that we could not distinguish who they were'.[26] This appears to be an exceptional condition endured by those who travelled in numbers, and helps to explain the repeated reference to excessive thirst in the narratives.

Mobility was a key requirement for the campaign in the west. Here the roads were very different. Maxwell reports that in this region

there were 'practically no roads at all'. When it rained they easily deteriorated into a quagmire and took a long time to recover, while winter
travel was almost impossible 'for there were very few roads and the
bogs were almost impassable'.[27] During this period there are many
accounts of travellers sinking into the bogs. In fact, the main road from
Castlebar suitable for regular carriage use was only opened in 1824.

But the military had barracks and other quarters as well as necessary supplies provided for them. To some extent these buffered the
hardship and fatigue imposed by the weather when on the march in a
way that rebels found difficult to match. But in the final days of the
campaign against Humbert the military had to endure some of the
same privations as their rebel counterparts with long forced marches in
very inclement weather without tents and with little food.[28] However,
when it came to the final conflict at Ballinamuck, the draining effect
of these hardships was less on the overwhelming force of the pursuer
than on the pursued.[29]

3. Weather and strategy in the war at sea: The weather at sea played a
major role in this conflict. Generally its significance has been overlooked because of the critical events that occurred in the land war. But
one of the most influential factors that affected the final outcome of
the rising was the absence of the French, and, when they did arrive,
their untimeliness. A principal reason for this was the wind and weather at sea and along the French coast that favoured the blockading
British fleet.

The wind conditions favouring the blockade of Brest were well
known and familiar to the fleet. The blockading fleet had to be constantly anticipating the changes, retreating to the shelter of the English
coast when severe westerly winds were expected, but quickly leaving to
take up station again when these passed, especially when the easterly
winds that would favour an exit from Brest, were expected. Always the
ships were seeking to have the weather gage (the windward position)
over its enemy in order to attack an enemy ship with the wind behind.

The advantage of the blockade was greater than merely shutting up
the French in Brest. While at sea there was constant opportunity for
training in gunnery and seamanship, including the speed of broadsides, the replacement of damaged masts and sails as well as experience
in a wide range of sea and weather conditions. In port there were few
opportunities for such practice. As a result the design superiority of the
French-built boats was cancelled out by the inexperienced seamanship
of the French crews.

A detailed knowledge of Brittany's coastal waters and how different weather conditions affected operational tactics there resulted from the long history of the Brest blockade. This began with Lord Hawke's blockade of 1759 when his officers and men gained as intimate a knowledge of the coastline as its inhabitants, and whose rocks and shoals, tidal and wind conditions worried many a captain to a shadow. This was passed on in the following decades, so that the response to even subtle weather changes became instinctive and the watch on Brest was never relaxed.[30]

Nevertheless, the events of 1798 demonstrated that it was possible to get past the blockade. The consequences of breaking out were still highly dependant upon the weather and the ability of the respective fleets to use the opportunities it presented. The superiority of the British fleet was reinforced by battle experience that confirmed its own self-belief. Recent significant sea battles had been won by the British fleet, particularly the 'Glorious First of June' in 1794, and in 1797 off Cape St Vincent and Camperdown.[31] In contrast, the French were dispirited and disorganised.[32] As a result, the main strategy of the French at sea was to avoid the English. In this they were very successful for most of the summer. They used the wind to take long, indirect routes, and the frequency with which they achieved this is evidence of a considerable level of seamanship and sea-weather awareness. Each of the French expeditions of 1798 avoided the blockade and made it to Ireland – from Rochelle (twice), Brest (although followed by frigates) and Dunkirk.

To invade Ireland the French intended to assemble an invading force at three different locations and make simultaneous attacks: Humbert from Rochelle, Hardy from Brest and twelve light craft from northern ports.[33] But this was fatally flawed by their ignorance of weather systems and their associated wind conditions, and in particular, how these varied over vast geographical areas. There are very few meteorological situations that would facilitate this strategy for such a diverse and lengthy coastline.

Storms at sea were a major hazard for all navies at this time. There was little ability to forecast these except for a short time ahead, even among the most experienced seamen. Losses of ships through bad weather was normally much greater than losses in battle or by capture. An invading fleet laden with hundreds of troops, artillery and equipment that weighed down their ships was very vulnerable. In a stormy sea or in a battle the lower gunports were often closed to keep the sea out. In desperate circumstances everything possible would be thrown overboard to gain speed and escape. The only advantage of having soldiers on board would come in close combat when their firepower and boarding capabilities would be useful.

There was a common belief that storms could occur at particular seasons and this sometimes influenced broad strategy. One of these was the equinox, when storms that were supposed to occur, not just at sea, but also on land. For example, Moore in his usual, careful way had planned to send his troops to their winter quarters just before the autumn equinox (21 September) when he heard of the *Anacreon's* landing. However, the season had become much less of a deterrent to action at sea and the French were prepared to risk having their invasion fleet at sea at this time. The French expected to be able to invade Ireland during the winter months and as early as April 1798 Bonaparte wrote of a plan to invade England in November or December of that year. However, the waters of the Channel were a different proposition to those around Ireland, especially in winter.

Even at sea, where strategy and tactics depended on the wind and a greater awareness of their vulnerability to the weather, strategic flair was in short supply.[35] There is not a great deal of evidence that the vast experience of weather at sea had been translated into knowledge that allowed weather sequences to be anticipated, except in the very short term. Tactics depended upon squeezing every advantage out of the prevailing conditions and using the weather opportunistically. Even Lord Howe, described by Nelson and most of his contemporaries as 'our great master in naval tactics', was not known for any greater understanding of the tactical possibilities of changing wind and weather conditions.[36]

THE WEATHER'S EFFECT ON THE EVENTS OF THE 1798 REBELLION: In earlier histories the weather of 1798 has been described in simple terms. At best, its treatment in the analysis of those events has been incomplete. This has led to a loss of detail and, in some instances, weaker explanations than are possible when its effects are more fully recognised and incorporated into our understanding of the rebellion.

The view that the weather was consistently dry and hot is based on faulty memory that at best was very partial. The coincidence of the security crisis and rebellion of May-June and to a lesser extent the initial French invasion in August with spells of comparatively dry and warm weather would certainly have made both occasions memorable. But even for this relatively short period it was probably the absence of rain rather than a combination of dryness and heat that facilitated the rebellion. In terms of outcomes the wind was also more frequently the significant critical factor determining the outcome of engagements between the protagonists than the summer heat. Of course, this was overwhelmingly so at sea.

There is little point in claiming that the weather favoured the rebellion. Of the events included in this account the insurgents gained some benefit over their enemies as a result of the weather on 58 occasions compared with 38 for the forces of the Crown. But its contribution was much more complex that that. It helped in giving the essential initial momentum to the rebellions in both May and late August. But even in the early days of the rebellion it also frequently cancelled out rebel advantages, especially their numerical advantage, which at times should have been overwhelming. Some of these occasions were at critical moments, such as at Arklow, where the larger strategic initiative was lost and was never recovered, and Ballynahinch which marked the end of the rebellion in Ulster. At sea the most significant weather influences were in helping to close up the French ports and in the battle of the Rosses. In both instances the weather acted overwhelmingly in favour of the British fleet.

On land these key actions can be regarded as largely moments of opportunity created by weather conditions that cancelled out an overwhelming advantage. At Arklow, Ballynahinch and (possibly) Goff's Bridge the vastly superior rebel numbers were cancelled out by a combination of wind and smoke. At Lacken they were dispersed by rain. But the opportunities needed to be seized by taking an appropriate initiative, as at Ballynahinch by Nugent (although it was not followed up by Needham at Arklow). This was even more so in the key events at sea. The French forces that would have provided the rebels with devastating firepower as well as overwhelming numbers, were bottled up in port by the westerly winds. Then, in the final significant act, serious storm damage was inflicted on the French even before the battle of the Rosses began.

But the weather also acted cumulatively through longer periods of consistent weather conditions. This included the dry, hot period of May-June that was most strongly developed in County Wexford where it helped to keep the rebellion together and offered the prospect of extending it beyond the county. To a lesser extent there was a similar, but shorter period in August-early September, which had different consequences because the terrain remained wet and the roads were inadequate when the joint French and Irish forces needed to move quickly. The contrasting wet, cold period of July-August was also exceptional and drove out the military forces from the rebels' most secure strongholds. But it also fatally undermined the rebels' resistance and many slipped away to take advantage of the pardons that were being offered by Cornwallis in his new strategy to bring the rising to a final conclusion.

The most famous event of 1798 is probably the 'Races of Castlebar' when the defending crown forces fled in disarray to Tuam and beyond. This achievement of Humbert was against all the odds. It defied any logic. Even the weather was against him, causing delay and the loss of surprise, which at the time appeared to be his only hope of success. But there were no certain outcomes in 1798. Even in that dark and bloody sequence of events, the possibility of supreme human determination, character and strategy overcoming all the conditions appearing to dictate a different outcome, was occasionally evident on both sides of the conflict. To that, even the dictates of the weather had to bow.

APPENDIX

Weather systems change from day to day as the air within them mixes and is modified by the surfaces over which they travel. However, there is a tendency for particular patterns and sequences of weather to result as they approach Ireland. The following simplified models show typical weather sequences for summer depressions (when atmospheric pressure is low) and anticyclones (when atmospheric pressure is high) that cross, or pass close to, Ireland. The depressions move much more quickly than anticyclones so the weather they bring may change rapidly over a few hours. Lingering anticyclones are much less

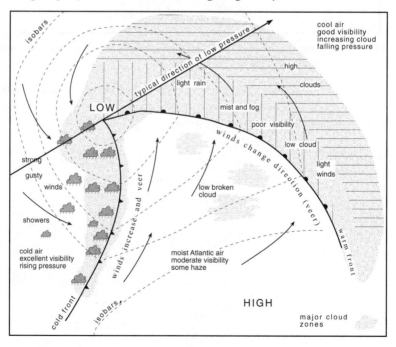

A generalised pattern of weather conditions typically experienced in a depression that crosses, or passes close to, Ireland.

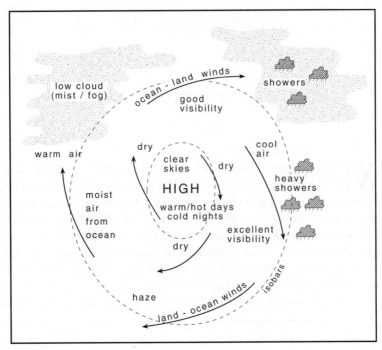

A generalised pattern of weather conditions typically experienced in an anticyclone over or close to, Ireland.

variable, although the contrasting weather that occurs around their periphery in the model shows that significant weather contrasts can be produced by small changes in position.

ENDNOTES

CHAPTER 1

1. Richard Hayes, *The Last Invasion of Ireland* (Dublin, 1937), p.322; Peter O'Shaughnessy (ed.), *Rebellion in Wicklow: General Joseph Holt's personal account of 1798* (Dublin, 1998).

2. John Joyce, *General Thomas Cloney: Wexford rebel of 1798* (Dublin, 1988), p.66.

3. Thomas Pakenham, *The Year of Liberty: the story of the great Irish rebellion of 1798* (London, 1969), p.212.

4. Eamon Doyle, *March into Meath* (Enniscorthy, 1997), p.6.

5. Peadar MacSuibhne, *Kildare in 1798* (Naas, 1978), p.204

6. Charles Dickson, *The Wexford Rising in 1798* (Tralee, 1955), p.72.

7. Pakenham, op. cit., p.156.

8. Ibid., p.212.

9. Danny Doyle and Terence Folan, *The Golden Sun of Irish Freedom: 1798 in Song and Story* (Dublin, 1998), p.128.

10. Ibid., p.99

11. Ibid., p.121.

12. Ibid., p.77.

13. Ibid., p.136.

14. Ibid., p.144.

15. Ibid., p.161.

16. Dudley Pope, *Life in Nelson's Navy* (London, 1981), p.83.

17. John Tyrrell, 'The Weather and Political Destiny', in John A. Murphy, *The French are in the Bay* (Cork, 1997), p.35.

18. Logbook of *Polyphemus*, Public Record Office, Kew, ADM 52/3299.

19. Logbook of *Princess*, Public Records Office, Kew, ADM 52/3318, 3319.

20. Logbook of *Dorset*, Public Records Office, Kew, ADM 52/2944, 2948.

21. Logbook of *Cerberus*, Public Records Office, Kew, ADM 52/2483.

22. The other 42 logbooks were from the following ships: *Actaeon, Amelia, Alcmene, Anson, Ariadne, Ardent, Anacreon, Bravo, Belliqueux, Caesar, Canada, Chapman, Dart, Diana, Doris, Dryad, Ethalion, Foudroyant, Ganges, Intrepid, Iris, Isis, La Legere, Lion, Lively, Lord Flood, Lancaster, Magnanime, Mahanesa, Melampus, Mercury, Meteor, Monmouth, Prince, Proselyte, Ranger, Repulse, Robust, Success, Sylph, Tisiphone, Vanguard.*

23. Alan Stimson 'The Longitude Problem: the Navigators Story' in William Andrewes (ed.), *The Quest for Longitude* (Cambridge, 1996), pp.71-84.

24. J. Butler and M. Hoskin, 'The archives of Armagh Observatory', *Journal for the*

History of Astronomy, xviii (1987), pp.295-307.

25. J. Hamilton, 'A letter to the Reverend Ussher DD from the Reverend James A. Hamilton DD, MRIA, giving an account of parahelia seen at Cookstown September 24, 1783' *Transactions of the Royal Irish Academy*, 1 (1787), pp.23-4.

26. J. Hamilton, 'On a new kind of portable barometer for measuring heights', *Transactions of the Royal Irish Academy*, 5 (1793-4), pp.95-107.

27. J. Butler and D. Johnson, 'A provisional long mean air temperature series for Armagh Observatory' *Journal of Atmospheric and Terrestrial Physics*, 58 (1996), pp.1657-1672.

28. Registry of the Weather, Belfast Society for Promoting Knowledge, unpublished.

29. Andrew Malcolm, *History of the General Hospital, Belfast* (Belfast,1851).

30. John Anderson, *History of the Belfast Library and Society for Promoting Knowledge* (Belfast, 1888), pp.19, 105-111.

31. In its original communicated form see 'On the weather of Derry in 1798 by Dr Paterson' Royal Irish Academy Ms 24Q26.

32. Harriet Butler and Harold Edgeworth Butler (eds), *The Black Book of Edgeworthstown and Other Edgeworth Memories 1585-1817* (London, 1927), p.60.

33. 'An abstract of observations of the weather of 1798, made by Henry Edgeworth, Esq., at Edgeworthstown in the County of Longford in Ireland', *Transactions of the Royal Irish Academy*, VII (1800), p. 317.

34. M. Donovan, 'Biographical account of the late Richard Kirwan Esq.', *Proceedings of the Royal Irish Academy*, IV(1847-1850), appendix VIII, pp.lxxxi-cxviii.

35. R. Kirwan, 'Synoptical view of the state of the weather at Dublin in the year 1798', *Transactions of the Royal Irish Academy*, VII (1800), p. 316.

36. H. Lloyd, 'Notes on the meteorology of Ireland, deduced from the observations made in the year 1851, under the direction of the Royal Irish Academy', *Transactions of the Royal Irish Academy*, XXII (1848-55), pp.417-498.

37. J. Kingston, 'Daily weather mapping from 1781', *Climatic Change,* 3 (1980), pp.7-36.

Chapter 2

1. For example, there is a report in the *Belfast Newsletter*, 1 June 1798 of 'remarkable large new potatoes which were dug in an open field' in County Wicklow. On 5 June added a further report that 'on the 1st inst. new potatoes were dug by Mr John Eakin of Muff [in County Londonderry] several of which weighed two ounces'.

2. Armagh register, op. cit. Small pressure differences between Armagh and Belfast result from a small difference in altitude between the two stations, otherwise their data closely mirror each other.

3. On anticyclonic days with clear skies in May, midday temperatures are up to 3^0C lower than the daily maximum temperatures, which normally occur in mid-afternoon. See Met Eireann, *Monthly Weather Report* Part III Hourly Values of Meteorological Elements (Dublin, various dates).

4. William Lecky, *History of Ireland in the Eighteenth Century* Vol. IV (London, 1892), p.427 records that this was constantly appealed to as clear proof of God's favour.

5. George Taylor, *A History of the Rise, Progress and Suppression of the Rebellion in County Wexford in the year 1798* (Dublin, 1829), p.87; F.W. Palliser, *The Irish Rebellion of 1798* (London, no date), p.165.

6. Thomas Graham 'Dublin in 1798: the Key to the Planned Insurrection' in Daire Keogh and Nicholas Furlong, *The Mighty Wave: the 1798 Rebellion in Wexford* (Dublin, 1996), p.77; Lecky, op. cit., p.320; John Mitchell, *The History of the Great Irish Rebellion of 1798* (Glasgow, 1890), p.79; Sir Richard Musgrave, *Memoirs of the Different Rebellions in Ireland* (Dublin, 1801), p.217.

7. Seamus Cullen, 'Conflict and Rebellion in North Kildare,' in Seamus Cullen and Hermann Geissel (eds), *Fugitive Warfare: 1798 in North Kildare* (Clane, 1998), p.12; Palliser, op. cit., p.78; Musgrave, op. cit., p.213.

8. Musgrave, op. cit. p.232.

9. Musgrave, op. cit. p.239.

10. Joyce, op.cit., p.5; Dickson, op.cit., p.52.

11. Miles Byrne, *Memoirs of Miles Byrne* (Shannon, 1972), vol. 1, p.38.

12. Constantia Maxwell, *Country and Town under the Georges* (Dundalk, 1949), p.130.

13. These illustrate the book by William Hamilton Maxwell, *History of the Irish Rebellion in 1798* (London, 1845).

14. *The soils of Wexford;* Thomas Pakenham, *The Year of Liberty: the Story of the Great Irish Rebellion of 1798* (London, 1969), p.152; Palliser, op.cit., p.105.

15. Brian Cleary, 'The Battle of Oulart Hill: Context and Strategy', in Keogh and Furlong, op.cit., p.87.

16. Daniel Gahan, *The People's Rising: Wexford 1798* (Dublin, 1995), p.39.

17. Idem, p.53.

18. Dickson, op.cit., p.72.

19. Gahan, op. cit., p.52.

20. Musgrave, op. cit., p.330; Palliser, op. cit., p.112.

21. Gahan, op. cit. p.54; Palliser, op. cit., p. 118. These conditions persisted since Cloney also reported that the following night was also calm and still (Joyce, op. cit., p.7).

22. Dickson, op. cit. p.72; Pakenham, op. cit., p.156.

23. *Caesar* log, 29 May.

24. Dickson, op.cit., p.232.

25. Joyce, op. cit., p.7.

26. See the Cruickshank cartoon of Vinegar Hill in Maxwell, op.cit. p.99; Pakenham, op. cit., p. 168; Palliser, op. cit., p.165.

27. Byrne op.cit., p.115.

28. Dickson, op. cit., p.246.

29. Ruan O'Donnell, *The Rebellion in Wicklow, 1798* (Dublin, 1998), p.211.

30. O'Donnell, Ibid., p.184.

31. Pakenham, op.cit., p.176; Dickson, op.cit., p.86.

32. Dickson, op.cit., p. 228.

33. Dickson, op.cit., p.80.

CHAPTER 3

1. *Caesar* log.

2. Pakenham, op.cit., p.248.

3. At Armagh and Belfast the midday temperatures fell by 17^0F and 10^0F respectively.

4. Measured as 0.073ins.

5. Dickson, op. cit., p.94.

6. Byrne, op.cit., p.87; Seamus de Val, *Bun Clodi* (Bunclody, 1966), p. 123.

7. Dickson, op.cit., p.94; Byrne, op.cit., pp.88, 90.

8. Palliser, op. cit., p.133.

9. Dickson, op.cit., p.100.

10. Maxwell, op.cit., p.110.

11. Measured as 0.18ins.

12. Belfast register, Armagh register, *Dorset* log, *Princess* log.

13. Joyce, op.cit., p.53; Pakenham, op.cit., p.207.

14. Dickson, op.cit., p.114.

15. Pakenham, op.cit., p.205.

16. Charles Teeling, *The History of the Irish Rebellion of 1798, A Personal Narrative* (Glasgow, 1828) p.240; H.F.B. Wheeler and A.M. Broadley, *The War in Wexford* (London, 1910), p.133.

17. Dinah Goff, *Divine Protection Through Extraordinary Dangers* (Dublin, 1871), p.16, quoted in Dickson, op.cit., p.123.

18. Armagh midday temperatures fell from 73^0F to 60^0F (23^0C to 16^0C approximately) between 6 and 7 June.

19. A.T.Q. Stewart, *The Summer Soldiers* (Belfast, 1995), p.72.

20. Pakenham, op.cit., p.219.

21. Bill Wilsdon, *The Sites of the 1798 Rising in Antrim and Down* (Belfast, 1998), p.111.

22. Charles Dickson *Revolt in the North: Antrim and Down in 1798* (Dublin, 1960), p.134; Wilsdon, Ibid., p.112.

23. Wilsden, op.cit., p.113.

24. At Armagh it was noted as a 'very fine and bright morn and day'.

25. Specific mention of the shadows is made in Teeling, op.cit., p.130.

26. O'Donnell, op.cit., p. 214; Dickson, op.cit., p.130; Gahan, op.cit., p.152.

27. The defeat at Tuberneering on 5 June had panicked the Arklow garrison to abandon the town for nearly two days. Gerard Hayes-McCoy, *Irish Battles* (London, 1980), p.286; Byrne, op.cit., p.125.

28. O'Donnell, op.cit., p.126.

29. Palliser, op.cit., p.159; G. Hayes-McCoy, 'The Topography of a Battlefield: Arklow 1798', *The Irish Sword*, 1 (1949-53), pp.51-56.

30. O'Donnell, op.cit., p.221.

31. Hayes-McCoy, *Irish Battles*, p. 303.

32. Gahan, op.cit., p.157.

33. O'Donnell, op.cit., p.221.

34. Hayes-McCoy, *Irish Battles*, p. 304.

35. Wilsden, op.cit., p.144.

36. Measured as 70^0F

37. Dickson, *Antrim and Down*, p.228.

38. Dickson, Ibid., p.224.

39. Between 12 and 13 June the small pressure fall from 30.07ins to 30.01ins was almost insignificant (a mere 2mbs from 1019 to 1017mbs) but it was part of a slow decline over several days. The corroboration usually available from the Belfast data is lacking because the curfew imposed by General Nugesnt prevented the Linen Hall

observer reaching his instruments.

40. The weather was 'uncommonly hot', Pakenham, op.cit., p.229.

41. Teeling, op.cit., p.203; Dickson, *Antrim and Down,* p.153; Wilsdon, op.cit., p.157.

42. Teeling, op.cit., p.212.

43. Gahan, op. cit., p. 18.

44. Armagh register, 17 June.

45. J.F.Maurice, *The Diary of Sir John Moore* (London, 1904), p.295.

46. Armagh pressure 19 June was the lowest since 16 May.

47. Belfast register. Measured as 0.38 ins.

48. Gahan, op.cit., p.191.

49. Art Kavanagh, *Battles of 1798* (Bunclody, 1997), p.69.

50. Gahan, op.cit., p.193.

51. James Alexander, *A Succinct Narrative of the Rise and Progress of the Rebellion in the County of Wexford, especially in the vicinity of Ross* (Dublin, 1800), p.103.

52. Archibald McClaren, 'A Minute Description of the Battles of Gorey, Arklow and Vinegar Hill', in Dickson, *Wexford Rising,* p.245.

53. Gahan, op.cit., p.191.

54. *Belfast Newsletter* 26 June, *Dublin Evening Post,* 19 June.

55. Gahan, op.cit., p.195.

56. Byrne, op.cit., p.178.

57. *Melampus* log.

58. Gahan, op.cit., p.195.

59. P. Kerrigan, 'The Naval Attack on Wexford in June 1798', *The Irish Sword,* 15 (1982-8), pp.198-9.

60. Maxwell, op.cit., p.104.

61. Armagh register, 18 June and 20 June. Midday temperatures fell from 70^0F to 57^0F. The fall at Belfast was of the same order, 71^0F to 61^0F.

62. Gardiner and Ryan, op.cit., p.87.

63. Maurice, op.cit., p.296.

64. Gahan, op.cit., p.199.

65. The bridge crossed the River Corock near Foulkesmills.

66. Gahan, op.cit., p.200

67. Joyce, op.cit., p.31.

68. Palliser, op.cit., p.94.

69. Dickson, *Wexford Rising,* p.161

70. Byrne, op.cit., p.167

71. Dickson, *Wexford Rising,* p.158; Lecky, op.cit., p.460.

72. *Melampus* log, 21 June.

73. *Lancaster* log, *Mercury* log, *Melampus* log and *Princess* log.

74. Joyce, op.cit., p.34.

75. Dickson, *Wexford Rising,* p.249.

76. Musgrave, op.cit., p.504.

77. O'Donnell, op.cit., p.249

78. Palliser, op.cit., p.219.

79. O'Donnell, op.cit., p.251.

80. Byrne, op.cit., p.224.

81. Byrne, op.cit, p.227.

82. Byrne, op.cit., p.225, Palliser, op.cit., p.219.

83. Belfast recorded 11.2mm (measured as 0.45ins).

84. Byrne,op.cit., p.265.

Chapter 4

1. Measured as 4.63 inches (Belfast), 3.31 inches (Dublin) and 6.37 inches (Edgeworthstown).

2. O'Donnell, op.cit., p.268.

3. Saunders Newsletter, 13 July 1798, in O'Donnell, op.cit., p.269.

4. *Caesar* log and *Robust* log.

5. Gahan, op.cit., p.272.

6. Byrne, op.cit., p.274.

7. Gahan, op.cit., p.273.

8. Doyle, op.cit., p.4.

9. Byrne, op.cit., p.281; Doyle, op.cit., p.4; Gahan, op.cit., p. 279; O'Donnell, op.cit., p.266.

10. Doyle, op.cit., p.9.

11. Byrne, op.cit., p.303; Doyle, op.cit., p.7.

12. Doyle. op.cit., p.7.

13. Gahan, op. cit., p.283.

14. O'Donnell, op.cit., p.278.

15. The surrender took place on 21 July. See Doyle, op.cit., p.12.

16. Pakenham, op.cit., p.275.

17. Doyle, op.cit., p.10.

18. Doyle, op.cit., p.14.

19. Doyle, op.cit., p.17.

20. O'Shaughnessy, op.cit., p. 49.

21. Doyle, op.cit., p.18.

22. *Dorset* log.

23. *Faulkner's Journal*, 14 July 1798.

24. Letter from Gough to Colonel Vereker in Doyle, op.cit., p.105.

25. Letter from Lt Colonel Gough to Colonel Vereker in Doyle, op.cit., p.105.

26. Holt says most of the men were intoxicated, O'Shaughnessy, op. cit., p.50.

27. O'Donnell, op.cit., p.282. O'Shaughnessy, op.cit., p.50.

28. O'Donnell, op.cit., p.282.

29. O'Shaughnessy, op.cit., p.51.

30. O'Donnell, op.cit., p.273.

31. Maurice, op.cit., p.306.

32. Gahan, op.cit., p.290; O'Donnell,op.cit., p.275.

33. Maurice, op.cit., p.306.

34. 'The fatigue and exposure to wet I had suffered in the course of service in Wicklow brought on a fever which confined me to my tent for a week and weakened me.' Maurice, op.cit., p.311.

35. Doyle, op.cit., p.37; Teeling, op.cit., p.279.

36. O'Donnell, op.cit., p.282; Doyle, op.cit., p.109.

37. Doyle, op.cit., p.38; O'Donnell, op.cit., p.282.

38. Maurice, op.cit., p.306, 311.

39. Maurice, op.cit., p.310.

40. Maurice, op.cit., p.309.

41. O'Donnell, op.cit., p.293.

42. Byrne, op.cit., p.308; O'Donnell, op.cit., p.294.

43. Maurice, op.cit., p.309.

CHAPTER 5

1. Pakenham, op.cit., p.298, p.300.

2. Mahon, *The Influence of Sea Power on History* (Boston, 1928), p.30.

3. Hayes, op.cit., p.6.

4. Henry Boylan, *Theobald Wolfe Tone* (Dublin, 1981), p.127; Rupert Coughlan, *Napper Tandy* (Dublin, 1976), p.122; Teeling, op.cit., p.300.

5. Teeling, op.cit., p.300.

6. Hayes, op.cit., p.16.

7. F. Van Brock, 'a Memoir of 1798', *The Irish Sword*, ix (1969-70), pp.192-206.

8. Coughlan, op.cit., p.126; Freyer Grattan, *Bishop Stock's 'Narrative' of the Year of the French, 1798* (Ballina, 1982), p.3.

9. *Cerberus* log. Bishop Stock also reported that they sailed 'three days against a north wind' – information, no doubt, from his French captors.

10. Bulmer Hobson (ed.), *Letters of Wolfe Tone* (Dublin, no date), p.128.

11. Grattan, op. cit., p. 5.

12. Hobson, op.cit., p.128.

13. Hayes, op.cit., p.13.

14. Hayes, op. cit., p.18.

15. Grattan, op.cit., p. 5; R.Hayes, 'An Officer's Account of the French Campaign in Ireland in 1798', *The Irish Sword*, 2(1955), p.110-118.

16. Belfast register. At Belfast pressure rose from 994mbs (29.33 inches) to 1025mbs (30.24 inches) between 23 and 24 August. There was a similar rise at Armagh.

17. Hayes, *An Officer's Account*, p.111.

18. Hayes, *Last Invasion*, p.28.

19. Hayes, *Last Invasion*, p.34.

20. Hayes, *Last Invasion*, p.36; Pakenham, op.cit., p.308; Royal Irish Academy, *Atlas of Ireland* (Dublin, 1979), p.24.

21. Hayes, *Last Invasion*, p.69; J.F. Quinn, *History of Mayo* (Ballina, 1993), p. 115.

22. Van Brock, op.cit., p.197.

23. Kilmaine weather register; Shevawn Lynam, *Humanity Dick Martin 'King of Connemara' 1754-1834* (Dublin, 1997), p.112.

24. Kilmaine weather register.

25. Pakenham, op.cit., p.317.

26. Hayes, *Last Invasion.*, p.70; Pakenham, op.cit., p.310.

27. Quinn. op.cit., p.126.

28. Teeling, op.cit., p.308.

29. *Doris* 36 guns, *Melampus* 36 guns, *Cerberus* 32 guns, *Hurler* 16 guns; *Fox* 12 guns.

30. Grattan, op.cit., p. 32; Jack Munnelly, *The French Invasion of Connaught* (Ballina, 1998), p.22.

CHAPTER 6

1. Palliser, op.cit., p.235.
2. Pakenham, op.cit., p.319.
3. O'Shaughnessy, op.cit., p. 66.
4. Hayes, *Last Invasion*, p.289.
5. Measured as 70°F.
6. At Neale, the Kilmaine register records an afternoon shower then very heavy rain in the evening.
7. Maurice, op.cit., p.318, 320.
8. The Kilmaine register records a 'very great wind' at night, while at Armagh the night had 'rain + wind' and the next morning 'high wind and flying clouds'.
9. Compare Hayes, *Last Invasion*, p.73 with Teeling, op.cit., p.307.
10. Maurice, op.cit., p.320. 'On the 3rd... about 5pm I was sent for by Lord Cornwallis. He had just received a report that the rebels had marched from Castlebar that morning at 4 am'.
11. For example, 'such a heavy rain as has seldom been experienced', John Jones, *Impartial Narrative of the most important engagements that took place during the Irish Rebellion* (Dublin,1798), p. 234.
12. Royal Irish Academy, op.cit., p.24.
13. Pope, op.cit., p.82.
14. *Ariadne* log, 2 September.
15. Coughlan, op.cit., p.124.
16. Hayes, *Last Invasion*, p.89; Maxwell, op.cit., p.240; Liam Kelly, *A Flame Now Quenched*, (Dublin, 1998) p.93.
17. Quinn, op.cit., p.127.
18. Teeling, op.cit., p.308.
19. Armagh register, 5 September.
20. *Cerberus* log, 5 September; *Repulse* log, 5 September.
21. Kelly, op.cit., p.93.
22. The Neale register records 'very hot with heavy showers'.
23. Maxwell, op cit, p.265.
24. Hayes, *Last Invasion*, p.118.
25. Kathleen Flynn and Stan McCormick, *Westmeath in 1798: A Kilbeggan Rebellion* (Westmeath, 1995), p.112.
26. Hayes, *An Officer's Account*, p.166.
27. Hayes, *Last Invasion*, p.112.
28. Kelly, op.cit., p.114.
29. Kelly, op.cit., p.107.
30. *The Times*, 16 September 1798.
31. Hayes, *Last Invasion*, p.297.
32. Van Brock, op.cit., p.202.
33. Hayes, *Last Invasion*, p.239
34. *Belliqueux* log, 7 September.
35. Coughlan, op.cit., p.125.
36. Armagh register, 13 September.
37. Coughlan, op.cit., p.129.
38. Coughlan, op.cit., p.134.

39. Pakenham, op.cit., p.300
40. Teeling, op.cit., p.336; Kerrigan, 'The Capture of the *Hoche* in 1798, *The Irish Sword*, 13 (1977-79), p.124.
41. Tyrrell, op.cit., p.29.
42. Hayes, *Last invasion, p.155.*
43. Coughlan, op.cit., p.143.
44. Coughlan, op.cit., p.145.
45. William James, *The Naval History of Great Britain* (London, 1847), p.124.
46. Grattan, op.cit., p.87.
47. Jack Munnelly, *The French Invasion of Connaught* (Ballina,1998), p.40.
48. Grattan, op.cit., p.90.
49. A total of 0.44 inches; Belfast register, 23 September.
50. Grattan, op.cit., p.88.
51. Munnelly, op.cit., p.41.
52. Grattan, op. cit., p. 40.
53. Pakenham, op.cit., p.335.
54. Mahan, op.cit., p.337.
55. James, op.cit., p.125, who says that Countess was then 'certain' the ships were bound for Ireland.

CHAPTER 7

1. James, op.cit., p.125.
2. John Mitchel, *The History of Ireland*, vol. 2 (Glasgow, 1890), p.34; Pakenham, op.cit., p.338; Teeling, op.cit., p.337.
3. James, op.cit., p.126.
4. James, op.cit., p.127.
5. P. Kerrigan, 'the capture of the *Hoche* in 1798', *The Irish Sword*, 13, 1977-79, p.124.
6. Anthony Price, *The Eyes of the Fleet* (London, 1990), p.26.
7. James, op.cit., p.129.
8. James, op.cit., p;131; Wolfe Tone, *The Life of Wolfe Tone Written by Himself and Completed by his Son* (Dublin, no date), p. 124.
9. James, op.cit., p.131.
10. Belfast pressure rose from 1011 to 1031mbs (29.85 to 30.44 ins) and also rose at Armagh and Neale.
11. James, op.cit., p.134.
12. Kerrigan, op.cit., p.124.
13. *Belfast Newsletter*, 16 October, 1798.
14. Armagh pressure was 983mbs (29ins) on the night of 14 October, rising to 992mbs (9.26ins) at noon.
15. James, op.cit., p.140. *The Belfast Newsletter*, 19 October, noted the high southerly wind that blew 'almost a hurricane'.
16. James, op.cit., p.142.
17. Wheeler and Broadley, op.cit., p.262.
18. F. van Brock, 'Dilemma at Killala', *The Irish Sword*, 8, 1967-68, p.261; R.B.Aldridge, 'The Journal of Captain Joseph Bull', *The Irish Sword*, 8 (1967-8), p.67.
19. Aldridge, Ibid., p.66

20. Grattan, op.cit., p.112.

21. This appears to have been confined to the west and northwest (Kilmaine register and log data).

22. Belfast recorded the lowest pressure since a severe storm on 30 January.

23. James, op.cit., p. 147.

24. Pope, op.cit., p.231.

25. Kerrigan, op.cit., p.124.

26. *Melampus* log. The journey of six days is shorter than the ten stated by James (p.136).

27. Teeling, op.cit., p.337.

CHAPTER 8

1. K. Douglas, H. Lamb, C. Loader, *A Meteorological Study of July to October 1588: the Spanish Armada Storms*. Climatic Research Unit Publication CRU RP 6 Norwich, 1978.

2. David Dickson, *Arctic Ireland* (Dublin, 1997), p.11; J. Tyrrell, 'Paraclimatic statistics and the Study of Climatic Change: the case of the Cork region in the 1750s', *Irish Geography*, 29 (1995), pp.231-245

3. *Census of Ireland for the Year 1851*, vol. 1, Section II, pp. 334-347.

4. Edward Wakefield, *An Account of the Ireland, Statistical and Political* (London,1812), p.186

5. Kirwan in *Census*, p.352.

6. Over five of the six years before 1798, for 21 of the 25 summer months rain fell on 50 per cent or more of their days.

7. Francois de Lactocnaye, *A Frenchman's Walk Through Ireland*, (Dublin, 1984) p.280.

8. de Lactocnaye, Ibid., p.53 and p.88.

9. de Lactocnaye, Ibid., p.87.

10. Belfast, Manchester and Rutland although not in northern areas such as Edinburgh, see J. Dalton, 'Meteorological Observations', *Memoirs of the Literary and Philosophical Society of Manchester*, 5,1(1802), pp.666-74.

11. Frieda Nicholas and J. Glasspoole, 'General Monthly Rainfall over England and Wales 1722 to 1931', *British Rainfall*, (1931) pp.299-306.

12. H. Lamb and A. Johnson, Secular Variations of the Atmospheric Circulation Since 1750, *HMSO Geophysical Memoirs* No.110 (London, 1966), p.110.

13. Wakefield, op.cit., p.191.

14. Measured as 3 and 9 degrees fahrenheit.

15. Quoted in MacSuibhne, op.cit., p.116.

16. Met Eireann, *Monthly Weather Bulletin*, June 1998, p.13.

17. Kevin Whelan, 'The role of the Catholic priest in the 1798 rebellion in County Wexford', in Kevin Whelan (ed.), *Wexford: History and Society*, Dublin 1987, p.309.

18. Taylor, op.cit., p.91; Hayes-McCoy, *Irish Battles*, p.288.

19. Teeling, op.cit., p.101 and p.108.

20. Myrtle Hill, 'the Religious Context; Protestantism in County Down in 1798', in Myrtle Hill, Brian Thrower and Kenneth Dawson, *1798 Revolution in County Down* (Newtownards, 1998), p.68.

21. Teeling, op. cit., p.200.

22. O'Shaughnessy, op.cit., pp.92, 110; MacSuibhne, op.cit., p. 120.

23. O'Donnell, op.cit., p.293.

24. Maurice, op.cit., p.316.

25. Maurice, op.cit., p.295.

26. McHugh, Roger (ed.), *Carlow in '98* (Dublin, 1949), p.149.

27. Maxwell, C., op. cit., p.284.

28. F.S.Bourke, 'The French Invasion of 1798: A Forgotten Witness', *The Irish Sword,* 2 (1954-56), p.29.

29. Liam Kelly, op.cit., p.121.

30. Oliver Warner, *Command at Sea: Great Fighting Admirals from Hawke to Nimitz* (London, 1976), p. 10.

31. E.H. Jenkins, *A History of the French Navy* (McDonald and Jane's, 1973), p.216; William James, *The Naval History of Great Britain,* vol.II (London,1837), p.46 and p.75; Denis Wheeler, 'The Weather During Admiral Duncan's North Sea Campaign: January-October 1797', *Meteorological Magazine,* 122, p.9 (1993).

32. Henry Boylan, *Theobald Wolfe Tone* (Dublin, 1981), p.124.

33. F. van Brock, 'Dilemma at Killala', *The Irish Sword,* 8, p.261 (1967-68).

34. James, op. cit., p.111.

35. Warner, op. cit., p.xii.

36. Warner, op. cit., p.65.

BIBLIOGRAPHY

Aldridge, R.B., 'The Journal of Captain Joseph Bull', *The Irish Sword*, 8 (1967-68)

Alexander, James, *A Succinct Narrative of the Rise and Progress of the Rebellion in the County of Wexford, especially in the vicinity of Ross* (Dublin, 1800)

Anderson, John, *History of the Belfast Library and Society for Promoting Knowledge* (Belfast, 1888)

Anon., *Census of Ireland for the Year 1851*, (Dublin,)

Bourke, F.S., 'The French Invasion of 1798: A Forgotten Witness', *The Irish Sword*, 2 (1954-556)

Boylan, Henry, *Theobold Wolfe Tone* (Dublin, 1981)

Butler, Harriet, and Butler, Harold Edgeworth, (eds), *The Black Book of Edgeworthstown and other Edgeworth Memories 1585-1817* (London, 1927)

Butler, J. and Hoskin, M., 'The archives of Armagh Observatory', *Journal for the History of Astronomy*, xviii (1987)

Butler, J., and Johnson, D., 'A provisional long mean air temperature series for Armagh Observatory' *Journal of Atmospheric and Terrestrial Physics*, 58 (1996)

Byrne, Miles, *The Memoirs of Miles Byrne* (Shannon, 1972)

Cleary, Brian, 'The Battle of Oulart Hill: Context and Strategy', in Keogh, Daire and Furlong, Nicholas, *The Mighty Wave: the 1798 Rebellion in Wexford* (Dublin, 1996)

Coughlan, Rupert, *Napper Tandy* (Dublin, 1976)

Cullen, Seamus, 'Conflict and Rebellion in North Kildare', in Cullen, Seamus and Geissel, Hermann (eds), *Fugitive Warfare: 1798 in North Kildare* (Clane, 1998)

Dalton, J. 'Meteorological Observations', *Memoirs of the Literary and Philosophical Society of Manchester*, 5, 1 (1802)

De Latocnaye, *A Frenchman's Walk through Ireland, 1796-7* (Dublin, 1984)

Dickson, Charles, *The Wexford Rising in 1798* (Tralee, 1955)

Dickson, Charles, *Revolt in the North: Antrim and Down in 1798* (Dublin, 1960)

Dickson, David, *Arctic Ireland* (Dublin, 1997)

Donovan, M., 'Biographical account of the late Richard Kirwan Esq.', *Proceedings of the Royal Irish Academy*, iv (1847-1850)

Douglas, K, Lamb, Hubert and Loader, C., *A Meteorological Study of July to October 1588: the Spanish Armada Storms* (Norwich, 1978)

Doyle, Danny and Folan,Terence, *The Golden Sun of Irish Freedom in Song and Story* (Dublin, 1998)

Doyle, Eamon, *March into Meath* (Enniscorthy, 1997)

Edgeworth, H., 'An abstract of observations of the weather of 1798, made by Henry

Edgeworth Esq. At Edgeworthstown in the County of Longford in Ireland', *Transactions of the Royal Irish Academy,* IV (1800)

Flynn, Kathleen and McCormick, Stan, *Westmeath in 1798: A Kilbeggan Rebellion* (Westmeath, 1995)

Gahan, Daniel, *The People's Rising: Wexford 1798* (Dublin, 1995)

Gardiner, Michael and Ryan, Pierce, *The Soils of County Wexford* (Dublin, 1964)

Goff, Dinah, *Divine Protection Through Extraordinary Dangers* (Dublin, 1871)

Graham, T., 'Dublin in 1798: the key to the planned insurrection', in Keogh, Daire and Furlong, Nicholas, *The Mighty Wave: the 1798 Rebellion in Wexford* (Dublin, 1996)

Grattan, Freyer (ed.), *Bishop Stock's 'Narrative' of the Year of the French: 1998* (Ballina, 1981), reprint of the 2nd edition (Dublin, 1800)

Hamilton, J., 'A letter to the Reverend Ussher DD from the Reverend James A. Hamilton DD, MRIA, giving an account of parahelia seen at Cookstown September 24, 1783', *Transactions of the Royal Irish Academy,* 1 (1787)

Hamilton, J., 'On a new kind of portable barometer for measuring heights', *Transactions of the Royal Irish Academy,* 5 (1793-4)

Hayes, Richard, *The Last Invasion of Ireland* (Dublin, 1937)

Hayes, R. 'An Officers Account of the French Campaign in Ireland in 1798', *The Irish Sword,* ii (1955)

Hayes-McCoy, G. 'The Topography of a Battlefield: Arklow 1798', *Irish Sword,* 1 (1949-53)

Hayes-McCoy, Gerard, *Irish Battles* (London, 1980)

Hill, Myrtle, Turner, Brian and Dawson, Kenneth, *1798 Rebellion in County Down* (Newtownards, 1998)

James, William, *The Naval History of Great Britain* (London, 1837)

Jones, John *Impartial Narrative of the most important engagements that took place during the Irish Rebellion* (Dublin, 1798)

Joyce, John, *General Thomas Cloney: Wexford rebel of 1798* (Dublin, 1988)

Kavanagh, Art, *Battles of 1798* (Bunclody, 1997)

Kelly, Liam, *A Flame Now Quenched* (Dublin, 1998)

Kerrigan, P. 'The Capture of the *Hoche* in 1798', *The Irish Sword,* 13 (1977-79)

Kerrigan, P., 'The Naval Attack on Wexford in June 1798', *The Irish Sword,* 15 (1982-88)

Kington, J., 'Daily Weather mapping from 1871', *Climatic Change,* 3 (1980)

Kirwan, R., 'Synoptical view of the state of the weather at Dublin in the year 1798', *Transactions of the Royal Irish Academy,* xxii (1848-55)

Lamb, Hubert, and Johnson, A., *Secular Variations of the Atmospheric Circulation Since 1750* (London, 1966)

Lecky, William, *History of Ireland in the Eighteenth Century* (London, 1892)

Lloyd, H. *Notes on the meteorology of Ireland, deduced from the observations made in the year 1851, under the direction of the Royal Irish Academy,* xxii (1848-55)

Lynam, Shevawn, *Humanity Dick Martin 'King of Connemara' 1754-1834* (Dublin, 1997)

McHugh, Roger, *Carlow in '98* (Dublin, 1949)

McSuibhne, Peadar, *Kildare in 1798* (Naas, 1978)

Mahon, A.T., *The Influence of Sea Power on History* (Boston, 1928)

Malcolm, Andrew, *History of the General Hospital, Belfast* (Belfast, 1851)

Maurice, J.F. (ed.), *The Diary of Sir John Moore* (London, 1904)

Maxwell, Constantia, *Country and Town under the Georges* (Dundalk, 1949)

Maxwell, William, *History of the Irish Rebellion in 1798* (London, 1845)

McClaren, Archibald, 'A Minute Description of the Battles of Gorey, Arklow and Vinegar Hill', in Dickson, *The Wexford Rising in 1798* (Tralee 1955)

Mitchell, John, *The History of the Great Irish Rebellion of 1798* (Glasgow, 1890)

Munnelly, Jack, *The French Invasion of Connaught* (Ballina, 1998)

Musgrave, Richard, *Memoirs of the Different Rebellions in Ireland* (Dublin, 1801)

Nicholas F. and Glasspoole J., 'General Monthly Rainfall over England and Wales 1722 to 1931', *British Rainfall* (1931)

O'Donnell, Ruan, *The Rebellion in Wicklow* (Dublin, 1998)

O'Shaughnessy, Peter, (ed.), *Rebellion in Wicklow: General Joseph Holt's personal account of 1798* (Dublin, 1998)

Quinn, J.F., *History of Mayo* (Ballina, 1993)

Pakenham, Thomas, *The Year of Liberty: the story of the great Irish Rebellion of 1798* (London, 1969)

Palliser, F.W., *The Irish Rebellion of 1798* (London, no date)

Pope, Dudley, *Life in Nelson's Navy* (London, 1981)

Price, Anthony, *The Eyes of the Fleet* (London, 1990)

Royal Irish Academy, *Atlas of Ireland,* (Dublin, 1979)

Stewart, A.T.Q., *The Summer Soldiers* (Belfast, 1995)

Stimson, A., 'The Longitude Problem: the navigator's story', in Andrewes, William, *The Quest for Longitude* (Cambridge, 1996)

Taylor, George, *A History of the Rise, Progress and Suppression of the Rebellion in County Wexford in the Year 1798* (Dublin, 1829)

Teeling, Charles, *The History of the Irish Rebellion of 1798, A Personal Narrative* (Glasgow, 1828)

Tone, Wolfe, *Life of Wolfe Tone Written by Himself and Completed by His Son* (Dublin, no date)

Tyrrell, J., 'Paramatic statistics and the study of climatiuc chnage: the case of the Cork region in the 1750s', *Climatic Change,* 29 (1995)

Tyrrell, J., 'The Weather and Political Destiny', in Murphy, John, *The French are in the Bay* (Cork, 1997)

Van Brock, F. 'Dilemma at Killala', *The Irish Sword,* 8 (1967-68)

Van Brock, F. 'A Memoir of 1798', *The Irish Sword,* 9 (1969-70)

Wakefield, Edward, *An Account of Ireland, Statistical and Political* (London, 1812)

Warner, Oliver, *Command at Sea: Great Fighting Admirals from Hawke to Nimitz* (London, 1976)

Wheeler, H.F.B., and Broadley, A.M., *The War in Wexford* (London, 1910)

Whelan, K., Wexford: History and Society (Dublin, 1987)

Wilsden, Bill, *The Sites of the 1798 Rising in Antrim and Down* (Belfast, 1998)

Wood, C.J. (ed.), *Journals and Memoirs of Thomas Russell, 1791-5* (Belfast, 1991)

INDEX

MORE TITLES FROM THIS PRESS

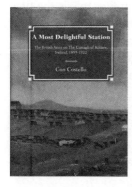

A Most Delightful Station
The British Army on the Curragh of Kildare, Ireland, 1855-1922
Con Costello

This is the first fully-documented account of the British Empire's most important training camp. The military of the Curragh became an essential part of the economic, social and sporting life of Kildare. Edward VII, Captain Oates of Scott's ill-fated Antarctic expedition, and Oswald Mosley received training at the Curragh. Its daily routines were later recalled by many writers including Maud Gonne and Seán Ó Faolain. A revealing portrait of the changing profile and role of a colonial army – officers, men and their families, it is based on original research and features much previously unpublished material.

1-898256-73-X   PB   £14.99   1999

Surplus People: The Fitzwilliam Clearances 1847-1856
Jim Rees

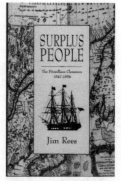

From 1847 to 1856, Lord Fitzwilliam arranged 'assisted passages' to Canada for 6,000 men, women and children from his 80,000-acre Coolattin Estate in Wicklow. Most were destitute on arrival in Quebec and New Brunswick. Despite good intentions there was terrible misunderstanding. This book describes the clearances and examines how some of the families fared in Canada. It also focuses on the infamous Grosse Île near Quebec.

1-898256-93-4   PB   £7.99   2000

The Heritage of Ireland

Edited by Neil Buttimer • Colin Rynne • Helen Guerin

A landmark in Irish studies, this is the first multidisciplinary approach to describe Ireland's complex heritage and analyse its protection and management. It is presented in three main parts: Natural, Man-Made and Cultural Heritage; Conservation and Interpretation; and Administration and Business. It will facilitate strategic planning at all levels and provides authoritative accounts of heritage legislation and EU institutions and directives dealing with heritage in the Republic of Ireland and Northern Ireland.

1-898256-15-2   PB   £25.00   2000
1-898256-80-2   HB   £50.00   2000

Companion Guide to Ireland

Brendan Lehane

In this revised and updated edition, an acknowl-edged expert concentrates on history, culture, architecture and art. This information-packed guide reads like the best of travel writing, always interesting and charming, sometimes eccentric.

1-903464-08-0 PB £15.00 colour b/w photos and maps 2001

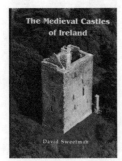

The Medieval Castles of Ireland

David Sweetman

Written by an eminent scholar and drawing on all the information available, including new data from recent excavation work, this is the most up-to-date study on Irish castles, tracing the development of the Irish medieval castle from 1169. It begins with the Anglo-Norman invasion and works through to the strong houses and fortified houses of the sixteenth and seventeenth centuries.

1-898256-75-6 HB £25.00 colour b/w photos and maps, line drawings   1999

Lord Kildare's Grand Tour 1766-1769

Elizabeth Fitzgerald

FOREWORD BY MOLLY KEANE

PREFACE BY KEVIN WHELAN

These intimate and tantalising letters, with an elegant commentary, provide fascinating reading today. Written by the young Lord Kildare to his mother Emily, Duchess of Leinster, they describe his experiences while on the Grand Tour. Not burdened with detailed descriptions of famous sites, galleries or churches, the letters indicate a sharp eye for social detail and a sense of humour: 'I forgot if I mentioned it ... but I had the honour of kissing the pope's toe (NB. It was very sweet).' Rome 1767.

The Duchess must have been satisfied the small fortune spent on her son's travel was not wasted. Throughout the rest of her life she treasured his letters.

1-898256-78-0   £12.99   2000

The Pleasing Hours: The Grand Tour of James Caulfeild, First Earl of Charlemont (1728-1799)
Cynthia O'Connor

The 1st Earl of Charlemont is best remembered today for having built the architectural masterpiece, the Casino at Marino, and Charlemont House, both in Dublin. He embarked on a Grand Tour from 1746 to 1754. In 1749 he sailed to Constantinople, Egypt, Asia Minor, the Greek Islands and Greece. His description of the Tour fizzles with excitement. He was founder member of the Royal Irish Academy and became its first president in 1785.

1-898256-66-7   HB   £20.00   1999